The Family Album

Compiled by Arthur and Nancy DeMoss

Since the first edition of *The Family Album* appeared in 1967, it has become a welcome source of joy and comfort to millions of people. Here the innermost thoughts and feelings of some of the world's most admired men and women are recorded as a priceless heritage, enhanced by stunning full-color photographs which appear throughout.

Young and old alike will return to these pages time and again to enjoy the works of celebrated authors like James Whitcomb Riley, Edgar Guest, Robert Frost, Henry Van Dyke, Edwin Markham, Eugenia Price, Charles Wesley, and Helen Lowrie Marshall. Here, too, are the words of such notables as Billy Graham, Peter and Catherine Marshall, Grandma Moses, and Dale Evans Rogers. In this edition a new section has been added called "Let's Read It Together" and is made up of selections which especially lend themselves to being read aloud.

This is a book to be cherished. The essays, anecdotes and poems are a gift of love and hope for people of all faiths. *The Family Album* is a gentle celebration of the beauty of God's earth, the wonder of God's creation.

The Family Album

Edited by
ARTHUR AND NANCY DeMOSS

Associate Editor
PHYLLIS HOBE

Published by
A.J. HOLMAN COMPANY
Division of J. B. Lippincott Company
PHILADELPHIA AND NEW YORK

ACKNOWLEDGMENTS

Grateful acknowledgment is hereby expressed to all those who have contributed to this book. Any inadvertent omissions of credit will be gladly corrected in future editions.

Elizabeth Anderson, "Child and Brook," from WHO TELLS THE CROCUSES IT'S SPRING. Reprinted by special permission of Farm Journal, Inc. Copyright © 1971, Countryside Press.

Jone Anderson, "My Act," from GOD, I LIKE YOU by Sherwood Wirt and Charlene Anderson. Copyright © 1962, 68, 69, 70, by The Billy Graham Evangelistic Assn. Reprinted with permission.

Molly Brooks, "What Christmas Is," from GOD, I LIKE YOU by Sherwood Wirt and Charlene Anderson. Copyright © 1962, 68, 69, 70, by The Billy Graham Evangelistic Assn. Used with permission.

Heywood Hale Broun, "The Shepherd Who Would Not Go," from THE COLLECTED EDITION OF HEYWOOD BROUN. Copyright © 1929, 1956 by Heywood Hale Broun and the Estate of Constance M. Broun. Used with permission.

Amy Carmichael, "Stay Thy Heart On Me," from EDGES OF HIS WAYS and a small passage which begins: "fragrance is like light . . . ." Reprinted by permission of The Society for the Publication of Christian Knowledge. Victor Cherbuliez, an excerpt from THE UNDERSTANDING HEART by Louise Bachelder. Reprinted with permission of Peter Pauper Press, Inc. Barbara Overton Christie, "Philosophy for Mothers," from WHO TELLS THE CROCUSES IT'S SPRING. Reprinted by special permission of Farm Journal, Inc. Copyright © 1971, Countryside Press.

Jule Creaser, "Prayer At Dawn," from GUIDEPOSTS. Reprinted by permission of GUIDEPOSTS MAGAZINE, copyright © 1969 by Guideposts Associates, Inc., Carmel, New York.

Grace Noll Crowell, "Might," and "Giving Thanks." Reprinted by permission of Reid Crowell.

"I Have Found Such Joy," from LIGHT OF THE YEARS. Copyright © 1936 by Harper and Row, Publishers, Inc.; renewed 1964 by Grace Noll Crowell. Used by permission of Harper and Row, Publishers, Inc.

"Let Us Be Quiet," from LET THE SUNSHINE IN. Reprinted by permission of Fleming H. Revell Company.

Ralph Spaulding Cushman, "Lonesome," from HILLTOP VERSES AND PRAYERS. Reprinted by permission of Abingdon Press.

Louise Darcy, "To Understand A Child," from HOME LIFE, July 1971. Copyright © 1971, The Sunday School Board of the Southern Baptist Convention. All rights reserved. Used by permission.

Annie Johnson Flint, "Passing Through," and "He Giveth More," from ANNIE JOHNSON FLINT'S BEST LOVED POEMS, and "The Christ of Calvary." Reprinted by permission of Evangelical Publishers, Canada.

(ACKNOWLEDGMENTS continued on page 176)

Contents

Editors' Foreword

Several years ago the Family Album was a personal collection of poetry and prose. As we came across these thoughts, stories and beautiful expressions that had a special meaning for the most important areas of life, we kept them and shared them with our family.

As our family grew, so did our collection. We began to share it with our friends, and at their urging it became the first edition of the Family Album.

This volume is the eighth edition. We pray it will bring you and all our friends—and you are also our "family"—the kind of spiritual comfort and joy it has given us from the beginning. May its contents convince you, as they have convinced us, that words offered to the glory of God are the most powerful and most beautiful in all the world.

Arthur and Nancy DeMoss
Valley Forge, Pennsylvania

The
Family Album

The New Year

Myself

I have to live with myself, and so
I want to be fit for myself to know;
I want to be able as days go by
Always to look myself straight in the eye;
I don't want to stand with the setting sun
And hate myself for the things I've done.

I don't want to keep on a closet shelf
A lot of secrets about myself,
And fool myself as I come and go
Into thinking that nobody else will know
The kind of a man I really am;
I don't want to dress myself up in sham.

I want to go out with my head erect,
I want to deserve all men's respect;
But here in the struggle for fame and pelf,
I want to be able to like myself.
I don't want to think as I come and go
That I'm bluster and bluff and empty show.

I never can hide myself from me,
I see what others may never see,
I know what others may never know,
I never can fool myself—and so,
Whatever happens, I want to be
Self-respecting and conscience free.

Edgar Guest

A Grace

For every cup and plateful,
God make us truly grateful.

A. S. T. Fisher

9

The Hidden Hand Of God

Life had become so meaningless and hopeless for William Cowper, the famous English poet, that he decided to commit suicide. Hailing a horse-drawn cab, he gave as his destination a bridge over the Thames River. But fog was so thick that night that he rode about for an hour or more. Where was the river? Rebuking the cabbie for taking so long to find the river bank, Cowper thrust open the door of his cab. Upon doing so, he discovered that instead of being near the river, he was right back at his own doorstep! Smitten by the coincidence, he rushed to his room, took a quill and paper and penned the lines that have cheered millions who have come to the brink of disaster:

> 'God moves in a mysterious way
> His wonders to perform;
> He plants His footsteps in the sea,
> And rides upon the storm.

Roy O. McClain

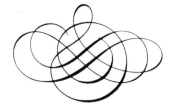

GOLDEN PRAYERS

Dear Lord...

Dear Lord, grant me Your peace. I do not ask for earthly peace which removes trouble or dulls the senses, but for that holy calm which never fails by day or by night, in joy or in sorrow, but ever lifts the soul to rest upon You. You were so peaceful Yourself, dear Christ, in Your life! Haste and worry and anxiety were never Yours, but a blessed calm which told of mastery. May it not be mine also? Speak to me, Lord. Bid the waves, which seem sometimes so big and threatening, to show themselves as under Your loving control. Touch my wearied heart, that it sink not in despair. Make me glad and brave and joyous always in the knowledge that I am Yours. And in all my ways lead me by Your own hand, and keep me in perfect peace. Amen.[3]

Floyd W. Tomkins

Remember This!

We must all have our quota,
Our portion and share
Of "crosses to carry"
And "burdens to bear"—
And no one knows God
Through joy alone,
It takes pain and suffering
To make us His own.

Helen Steiner Rice

The important thing is to know how to take all
things quietly.

Michael Faraday

The Challenge Of Resistance

No doubt a world in which matter never got out of place and became dirt, in which iron had no flaws and wood no cracks, in which gardens had no weeds, and food grew already cooked, in which clothes never wore out and washing was as easy as the soapmakers' advertisements describe it, in which rules had no exceptions and things never went wrong, would be a much easier place to live in. But for purposes of training and development it would be worth nothing at all.

It is the resistance that puts us on our mettle: it is the conquest of the reluctant stuff that educates the worker. I wish you enough difficulties to keep you well and make you strong and skillful!

Henry Van Dyke

Psalm 8

O Lord our Lord, how excellent is thy name in all the earth! who hast set thy glory above the heavens. Out of the mouth of babes and sucklings hast thou ordained strength because of thine enemies, that thou mightest still the enemy and the avenger. When I consider the heavens, the work of thy fingers, the moon and the stars, which thou hast ordained; what is man, that thou art mindful of him? and the son of man, that thou visitest him? For thou hast made him a little lower than the angels, and hast crowned him with glory and honour. Thou madest him to have dominion over the works of thy hands: thou hast put all things under his feet: All sheep and oxen, yea, and the beasts of the field; the fowl of the air, and the fish of the sea, and whatsoever passeth through the paths of the seas. O Lord our Lord, how excellent is thy name in all the earth!

Golden Thoughts

The doors of wisdom are never shut.

Benjamin Franklin

We are here to add what we can to, not to get what we can from, Life.

Sir William Osler

Common sense is a personal compass for guidance around the rocks and shoals of life.

D. A. Peterson

January Snow

The heart leans on its silence,
And God, with a gentle hand
Writes with the chalk of winter
On the blackboard of the land.

Alma Robison Higbee

Lonely Farm

The whirling snow, like huge, white petals blown
From heaven's tree, lay piled on fence and road.
The house was old and gray, and all alone,
And past it, storm-winds, roaring hoarsely, strode.

The fields were harvested, and now lay bare.
It seemed a wild, deserted place to me,
That windy evening through the frosted air,
A sad old house beneath a leafless tree.
But, when I entered—what a change I found!

The farmer sat within a clean, warm room,
A rugged man whom summer days had browned.
In catalogues, he read when plants would bloom,
And talked of fertile fields, of sun and seed,
And all the hungry that his land could feed.

Lois Kingsley Pelton

My Pilot

Ships coming into port slow down to "pick up the pilot"—to take aboard a man who knows every rock and sand bar in the harbor and who can steer the ship safely through them to the dock. When the ship leaves the harbour, the same pilot comes aboard to take her out to deep water and the open sea, and then they "drop the pilot."

"Dropping the pilot" has always made me sad, whether it happens on a ship or in a human life, but "picking up the pilot" always thrills me. "Jesus, Saviour, Pilot me," I sang as a child, and it means more to me now that I have put away childish things. I suppose I picked up and dropped a dozen pilots for my life's voyage, before He came to guide me. Don't we all? When the boy is six he wants to be a fireman; at ten he would be either a cow-puncher or president; at fifteen an astronaut, then a lawyer, doctor or minister. We all pick out our heroes and worship and imitate them—dream that we may be like them when we grow up. We'd save a lot of trouble and frustration if we would pick up Christ as our Pilot while we are still young. Why must we wait half a lifetime before taking Him aboard?

I say there is no better pilot, for He has been at it longer. He was here with the first of men and even before that; He said, "Before Abraham was, I am." He was here before Abraham was here. "For by him were all things created, that are in heaven, and that are in earth, visible and invisible, whether they be thrones, or dominions, or principalities, or powers: all things were created by him, and for him: And he is before all things, and by him all things consist" (Colossians 1:16-17). God in Christ *created* us; could you think of one better able to guide us?

One of the Russian astronauts said he looked out of the window of his little spaceship, up there in space, and he didn't see any angel, or any heaven, or any God. Poor little man! He was looking the wrong way in the wrong place. You can't see an atom either, but you know it's there, because we've put it to work. God made the atom and He made us, and He has made them work together, and if the atheist in the space capsule had looked a little more intelligently at man he'd have seen God at work, and heaven in the human heart. He can still find plenty of Christ-guided men, if he wants to look . . .

We belong to this God in Christ, for He created us. Without Him, we are nothing. He is our next heartbeat. Before the earth was formed and after it shall have disappeared, Jesus *is*. He has always been and always will be, even after we stupid "scientists" have used His atom to blow our earth to bits. Only when we realize this and turn to Him and put *all* our trust in Him can we live life to its fullest. The most interesting and inspiring people I have met, the most *alive* people, have been dedicated Christians. I've known some outstanding Christian doctors, musicians, athletes, teachers, scientists (yes, scientists!), writers and businessmen who have taken Christ into their lives and they vibrate with His loving and dynamic power. If that's what you are looking for—power to live—I suggest you reach out and touch Him. . . .

Look at this Christ! Born in a stable when He might have been born in a palace, He was a King in a carpenter's house, in the home of obscure Joseph and Mary. He was not educated in the schools as our children are, yet at twelve He had a wisdom so profound that He was an amazement to the teachers in the temple at Jerusalem. He was implicitly obedient to Joseph and Mary though He had power from His Father in heaven to still the waves and the storms of the human heart. He fed thousands with five loaves and two fishes; He healed with the mere touch of His hand and He raised more than one from the dead.

He was no weakling, this Christ. He was strong. In the carpenter shop at Nazareth He lifted long heavy beams of wood and did hard labor without benefit of machinery and electric tools. He walked long miles in the hot and dusty roads of Judea and Galilee, on errands of healing and pity, asking no pay but the following of His Way and truth. Strong Himself, He knew well that most of us would be too weak to follow Him as we should, too weak to win His everlasting life by any efforts of our own, so in the end, He paid the price for our weakness and selfishness as He offered His blood to wash it all away, at the cross. He died there for multitudes of us whom He had never seen, yet loved.

Some thought it was all over when He died; they smiled, "Well, that's the last of *Him!*" It wasn't. The third day He rose and walked out of the tomb where they had laid Him, God in the flesh of man, proving that there was a life beyond the tomb for other men, bought for them on that cross. Then He went to sit at the right hand of His Father, to intercede for us with Him. . . .

This then is Jesus called the Christ. This is what He was, and what He did. This is the brief account of His brief, matchless life; even His worst enemies wonder at it and admit the glory and the power in it. I believe in Him, I believe all this about Him, not so much because I want to but because I have to. The evidence that He is all this and did all this is too strong for me to doubt. I believe that He is the Word, that it is He of whom John speaks when he tells of the Word being made flesh. I believe He is the Lamb without spot whom the prophet predicted would come; I believe He is God's only Begotten, come to save. I believe it because He has saved me.

Often I am overwhelmed with the immensity of it all, and I feel completely inadequate and unworthy of such a Saviour, and unable to explain any of it. So much of the story of Jesus—the incarnation, the works of wonder, the resurrection—is too much for my small heart. I cannot grasp their full meaning, cannot begin to explain the mysteries involved. I am no trained theologian, but this I do know: though the mystery remains, Jesus Christ has led me as a shepherd leads his uncomprehending sheep. He leads me in not just great moments of blazing crisis, at the great crucial moments of decision in my life, but—which may be more important—He leads me every day, every hour, in every little moment on the road I walk.

Dale Evans Rogers

Easter

I walked today where Jesus walked,
  When to the wilderness He fled.
I followed in the path He took,
  When in Gethsemane He prayed.

The stony pathways that He trod
  To heal the sick, the lame, the blind,
I took today and as I walked
  I sought His gentle love to find.

When unto Pilate He was led,
  The purple robe and thorns to wear,
I walked today and wished I might
  His load of grief and sorrow share.

My footsteps faltered when I tried
  Golgotha's rugged hill to climb.
He hesitated not at all
  And paid in suffering for my crime.

If in our Saviour's steps we'd walk,
  Our lives in service give to Him,
The stones and thorns we must accept,
  Nor shun the cross, nor ardor dim.

Virginia Hibbard

Golden Nuggets

The breath of God
Stirs to life the green and growing things
That sleep beneath the sod.
He breathes on me
And in each resurrected flower
The Living Christ I see.

Myra Brooks Welch

An Easter Miracle

In the year 1799, when Napoleon's armies were passing over Europe conquering all before them, they appeared on the heights above the town of Feldkirch, a force 18,000 strong, under the command of General Massena. The council of the little Austrian town hastily assembled and decided to send a deputation to Massena with the keys of the town and a petition for mercy. It was Easter morning. Mid the confusion, the old dean of the church spoke up, with no fear in his heart. "It is Easter morning," he said. "We have reckoned on our own strength, and it is weakness. Let us ring the bells and have services as usual. We will commit our troubles to a Higher Power."

Soon all the bells of the town were set ringing joyously. The streets thronged with worshipers on their way to church. Louder and more triumphantly rang the bells with the victorious Easter message. The French heard the sounds of rejoicing, and Massena concluded there could be only one reason for it. The Austrian army must have come up in the night. He ordered camp to be broken, and long before the Easter services were over, the French army was in retreat.

By noon not a tent, not a soldier, not a glittering bayonet was to be seen. Feldkirch was saved.

Sunshine Magazine

GOLDEN THOUGHTS

The most important events in human history are the death and resurrection of Jesus Christ.

Billy Graham

Fulfillment

Apple blossoms bursting wide
   now beautify the tree
And make a Springtime picture
   that is beautiful to see . . .
Oh, fragrant lovely blossoms,
   you'll make a bright bouquet
If I but break your branches
   from the apple tree today . . .
But if I break your branches
   and make your beauty mine,
You'll bear no fruit in season
   when severed from the vine . . .
And when we cut ourselves away
   from guidance that's divine,
Our lives will be as fruitless
   as the branch without the vine . . .
For as the flowering branches
   depend upon the tree
To nourish and fulfill them
   till they reach futurity,
We too must be dependent
   on our Father up above,
For we are but the *branches*
   and He's *the Tree of Love.*

Helen Steiner Rice

Sins Of Omission

I saw before me a mountain
   High and rocky through my tears,
Each rock a sin of omission
   Piled up by me through the years.

A mountain so dark and high
   It hid from me my Saviour's face,
Until He extended me His hand
   And saved me by His grace.

Maude P. Durfee

Saviour

Princely Jesus
clothed in flesh
walked as man
breathed as God
sacrificed as Saviour
died as sin
arose as Christ
   Jesus,
God's budded almond rod
grafting heaven's fragrance
   into reclaimed men
     hallelujah
     glory.

Rachel G. Rice

To Know Him Who Is True

If one of them remembered, Mary did.
If one of them said on earth's
   longest day,
"Why are we desolate? We heard Him bid
Us trust that He would rise, and show
   the way . . ."
It was His mother, surely. But
   they turned
Their pitying faces from her, and
   were still,
Remembering only the despair that burned
Into their hearts upon Golgotha's hill.
And so she pondered these things through
   the night
Within her heart, and through the night
   they shed
Their hopeless tears. And when in
   dawning light
They told her, "He is risen!" I think
   she said,
As mothers since the world began
   have done,
"I knew it would be so. I knew my Son."

Jane Merchant

The Face Of The Baby

The camel tracks made a path, clearcut and white, across the sands of the desert—the youngest thief, reining in his horse, was amazed at the depth, the clean definition of them. "The caravan must have been heavily laden," he said slowly and regretfully.

The thief of the band was not listening or even looking at the marks that wandered off toward the horizon line, but was staring into the heavens. "There is a strange, almost unearthly light coming from above," he said at last. "Perhaps it's an omen. Maybe it's just as well that we were too late."

The youngest thief laughed. "So, the shrine of a single star has worried and scared my brave master!" This experienced band had heard of a rich caravan coming from a far country to bring gifts to a king. But somehow their calculations had gone awry, and they had reached the appointed place too late; the caravan had passed. They could, as the youngest thief had pointed out, chance overtaking the laden camels before the safety of the town had been reached, but if the town were entered the hard riding and crafty planning would be wasted. Once inside of the town the caravan and the gifts it bore would be safe. No thief with a price on his head enters a city's walls.

The leader rode first, but the youngest thief was aware of the droop in his master's shoulders. Well did he and the others of the band know that the strange starlight had bothered their chief.

Then the youngest thief sighted the caravan. "See, he cried. "We will overtake them." The chief of the band turned his weary eyes upon his young follower. "We will not overtake them," he said. "The town is but a short space away."

"I am not so easily discouraged," the youngest thief retorted. "I'll go on alone." His horse, feeling the touch of his spurs, leaped forward to follow the camel tracks that glimmered in a path of silver light. Only when he came into the outskirts of the little town did the youngest thief dismount from his horse. Putting on a brave front he advanced to the inn door and addressed the host who stood on the threshold. "I seek rest," said the youngest thief. But the host threw his hands apart, helplessly answering, "There is no room at the inn."

The youngest thief hesitated and then questioned, "May I at least stable my horse?" "The stable is also jammed," said the host.

Angrily the youngest thief turned away, crowding himself past a group of servitors dressed in rich livery. One of these the youngest thief approached. "Your master is a great man who seeks a king, does he not? And he is bearing gifts?"

Continued on Page 24

Continued from Page 23

The servitor was tired as well as preoccupied. He answered crossly. "A star led us across plains and mountains and deserts. We met two other princes on the way. And then, finally, we came into this town and the star pointed our destination to a stable." He laughed, "A fine place, one would say, in which to house a king."

The youngest thief made his way to a window on the side of the stable. With a throb of growing excitement he laid his hands upon the sill, raised his eyes and focused their glance on the interior room. Certainly he hadn't thought that he would see a prince in the rich robes of state kneeling, while two other princes waited their turn before a woman, a shabby woman with a baby in her arms.

The Prince, still kneeling, opened a casket filled with gold. For one instant only the youngest thief remembered his errand. His mind, soul, and body were groping forward that he might see the baby's face.

All at once the youngest thief thought different thoughts from those he had ever dared think about. He thought of green fields and crystal streams and hilltops gay with early sunshine. He thought of a living earned decently and honestly; of men looking unfurtively into the eyes of their fellows. Suddenly he prayed unconsciously and wordlessly to a God that he did not recognize.

It was then that he knew his mission had been quite forgotten and that he would never return to the band of desert thieves.

Life is often a desert path that winds wearily across a lonely road and the youngest thief found it so. Unequipped for the practical ways of earning a living, he fared badly in his new role of honest man. His hands, agile and quick at loosening a money belt, were unbelievably slow at the many tasks that required much less skill.

Thirty years passed and he remained untouched by the hand of friendship and understanding while a rumor was spreading through the countryside. It was a rumor of a leader who helped those that knew sickness of body and soul and who gave happiness to those forgotten of men. But the youngest thief did not hear these rumors in his travels.

It couldn't go on—not forever—a man must eat. The youngest thief, hysterical with hunger, began to beg in a market place. If they had only listened. If the man with the bulging pouch at his side had only answered kindly.

The youngest thief could almost smell the money this man's pouch contained. The youngest thief, following him, saw everything through a red haze. The trees and houses reeled like figures in a crimson dance. The rich man had pushed him aside and he was hungry. He followed him through streets and at a crossroad laid his hand upon the rich man's sleeve. "I'm starving," he pleaded.

The pudgy man surveyed the youngest thief. The word he said as one hand fondled the pouch was ugly, and again the trees began to sway in a red haze.

Like a man in a dream the youngest thief stopped and groped weakly in the dust, feeling the smooth sides of a stone. It was heavy to lift but it grew lighter as the pudgy man laughed contemptuously. His laughter stopped when the stone crashed suddenly into his sneering face.

They sentenced him to be crucified according to the law of honest people (which does not always take into consideration the fact that a man is starving).

Three crosses were upon the hilltop, and each of the crosses bore a burden of pain. On the one farthest from the youngest thief hung another robber, who spoke a stream of blasphemy. Between the two of them was pinioned a man with a finely sensitive face, a man who wore upon his brow a crown which had been fashioned of thorns.

There was a stirring at the foot of the middle cross. Men and women were crying and soldiers fought among themselves. But a curious lassitude crept over the body and into the brain of the youngest thief. He did not heed the words that were said until suddenly the man upon the middle cross spoke. His voice was so gentle, so touched with the wonder of eternal love that the youngest thief tried to listen through his swooning senses and numbed limbs.

The man on the middle cross spoke. "Father, forgive them, for they do not know what they do."

To the youngest thief the voice of the man brought a sudden realization. This man being crucified was asking that his tormentors be forgiven. Perhaps that was the answer: People, when they hurt other people, did not understand.

Surely, the youngest thief told himself, had they looked into his heart, the years would not have been so bitter. Surely, had they looked into his striving soul, the world would have trusted and helped him.

The robber on the far cross spoke in a tone drenched with hatred. "If thou be Christ, save thyself and us."

The name of Christ was unknown to the youngest thief. But suddenly he found himself speaking phrases of rebuke to the taunting robber. And as he spoke, he turned his head with a final effort to gaze upon the man beside him. It was then that he saw words printed upon the middle cross, above the man's head, reading "This is the King of the Jews."

Using his final courage, he spoke once more, slowly, "Lord, remember me when thou comest into thy kingdom."

The man on the middle cross turned his head until his eyes were level with the eyes of the youngest thief. And as their glances crossed the youngest thief knew that he had met with friendship and faith. As his eyes closed the youngest thief saw a stable and a baby resting against a mother's breast.

Someone, glancing up from the crowd below, saw with amazement and unbelief that a smile lay upon the still lips of the youngest thief.

Margaret E. Sangster

This EasteR Day!

Has there been a resurrection
    In your heart this Easter morn;
Have you ris'n o'er the doubts and fears
    That have made you so forlorn?
Have you cast aside the garments
    That have bound you day by day,
For a wondrous robe of glory
    And of righteousness for aye?

Has there been a resurrection
    From the death of sin and shame;
Have you left the tomb forever,
    A dear Saviour's love to claim?
Then, oh, pilgrim, you can tarry
    With great peace this Easter Day
Till you rise to be with Jesus
    In His realm of love for aye!

Author Unknown

Jesus Christ is not a crutch, He is the ground to walk on. √

Leighton Ford

GOLDEN NUGGETS

He Is Risen!

"He is risen" the angel told the women at the tomb on that first glad Easter morning. And they went forth to repeat the wonderful words to everyone they met. "Christ is risen! He is risen indeed!"

Today we, too, can know that same joy and wonder, if, from the door of our old sins and sorrows, we find Him risen in our hearts.

Esther Baldwin York

O God, Our Help

O God, our help in ages past,
    Our hope for years to come,
Our shelter from the stormy blast,
    And our eternal home:

Beneath the shadow of Thy Throne
    Thy saints have dwelt secure;
Sufficient is Thine arm alone,
    And our defence is sure.

Before the hills in order stood,
    Or earth received her frame,
From everlasting Thou art God,
    To endless years the same.

Thy word commands our flesh to dust,
    "Return ye sons of men":
All nations rose from earth at first,
    And turn to earth again.

A thousand ages in Thy sight
    Are like an evening gone;
Short as the watch that ends the night
    Before the rising sun.

Time, like an ever-rolling stream,
    Bears all its sons away;
They fly forgotten, as a dream
    Dies at the opening day.

Our God, our help in ages past;
    Our hope for years to come;
Be Thou our guard while troubles last,
    And our eternal home!

Isaac Watts

Remember

Whenever you know a desolate hour
And are steeped in misery,
Remember Christ was lonely too,
In bleak Gethsemane;
Whenever you feel that all of the world
Has turned its back on you,
Remember that Christ knew what it was
To feel abandoned too.

Whenever you feel that your burden
Is greater than you can bear,
Remember He too heartbreakingly knew
A moment of dark despair;
And remembering these things just bear in mind
His victory was finally won
When He bowed His head and humbly said,
"But Thy will, not Mine, be done!"

Author Unknown

John 10: 7-18

Then said Jesus unto them again, Verily, verily, I say unto you, I am the door of the sheep. All that ever came before me are thieves and robbers: but the sheep did not hear them. I am the door: by me if any man enter in, he shall be saved, and shall go in and out, and find pasture. The thief cometh not, but for to steal, and to kill, and to destroy: I am come that they might have life, and that they might have it more abundantly. I am the good shepherd: the good shepherd giveth his life for the sheep. But he that is an hireling, and not the shepherd, whose own the sheep are not, seeth the wolf coming, and leaveth the sheep, and fleeth: and the wolf catcheth them, and scattereth the sheep. The hireling fleeth, because he is an hireling, and careth not for the sheep. I am the good shepherd, and know my sheep, and am known of mine. As the Father knoweth me, even so know I the Father: and I lay down my life for the sheep. And other sheep I have, which are not of this fold: them also I must bring, and they shall hear my voice; and there shall be one fold, and one shepherd. Therefore doth my Father love me, because I lay down my life, that I might take it again. No man taketh it from me, but I lay it down of myself. I have power to lay it down, and I have power to take it again. This commandment have I received of my Father.

John 10:7-18

Stay Thy Heart On Me

I am the God of the stars,
They do not lose their way,
Not one do I mislay,
Their times are in My hand,
They move at My command.

I am the God of the stars,
Today as yesterday,
The God of thee and thine,
Less thine they are than Mine;
And shall Mine go astray?

I am the God of the stars,
Lift up thine eyes and see
As far as mortal may
Into Eternity;
And stay thy heart on Me.

Amy Carmichael

GOLDEN THOUGHTS

Our Lord has written the promise of the resurrection, not in books alone, but in every leaf in springtime.

Martin Luther

The Christian on his knees sees more than the philosopher on his tiptoes.

Unknown

He Giveth More Grace

He giveth more grace when the burdens grow greater,
He sendeth more strength when the labors increase;
To added affliction He addeth His Mercy
To multiplied trials, His multiplied peace.

His Love has no limit; His grace has no measure;
His power no boundary known unto men;
For out of His infinite riches in Jesus
He giveth and giveth and giveth again.

Annie Johnson Flint

An Easter Prayer

O God of Easter, God of resurrection power,
Bring heavenly life to our earthbound souls;
Thou, who did'st call Lazarus forth from his tomb,
Call us forth from dead works, and let our hearts be
    aglow with immortal glory and power.
Call us out of the tomb of hollow profession,
Of cold creeds, and wordy ritual,
And let thy life abundant permeate and saturate our
    stagnant souls,
Bringing joy where there is heaviness of heart,
Bring peace where there is confusion;
Bring love where there is bitterness;
And may we henceforth live in the glorious glow of
The Life which that first Easter poured forth upon a
    world of darkness.
And may we always be mindful of the Source of this
    life-giving power,
And come to Thee regularly to be refilled.
In the Savior's name,
Amen.

Author Unknown

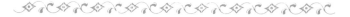

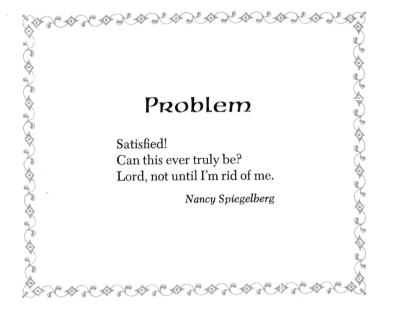

Problem

Satisfied!
Can this ever truly be?
Lord, not until I'm rid of me.

Nancy Spiegelberg

The Word Of The Cross

Look on thy God, Christ hidden in our flesh.
A bitter word, the cross, and bitter sight:
Hard rind without, to hold the heart of heaven.
Yet sweet it is; for God upon that tree
Did offer up His life: upon that rood
My Life hung, that my life might stand in God.
Christ, what am I to give Thee for my life?
Unless take from Thy hands the cup they hold,
To cleanse me with the precious draught of death.

What shall I do? My body to be burned?
Make myself vile? The debt's not paid out yet.
Whate'er I do, it is but I and Thou,
And still do I come short, still must Thou pay
My debts, O Christ; for debts Thyself hadst none.
What love may balance Thine? My Lord was found
In fashion like a slave, that so His slave
Might find himself in fashion like his Lord.
Think you the bargain's hard, to have exchanged
The transient for the eternal, to have sold
Earth to buy Heaven? More dearly God bought me.

Paulinus of Nola

I Looked

I looked upon a farm one day,
    That once I used to own;
The barn had fallen to the ground,
    The fields were overgrown.

The house in which my children grew,
    Where we had lived for years—
I turned to see it broken down,
    And brushed aside the tears.

I looked upon my soul one day,
    To find it too had grown
With thorns and nettles everywhere,
    The seeds neglect had sown.

The years had passed while I had cared
    For things of lesser worth:
The things of Heaven I let go
    While minding things of Earth.

To Christ I turned with bitter tears,
    And cried, "O Lord, forgive!
I haven't much time left for Thee,
    Not many years to live."

The wasted years forever gone,
    The days I can't recall;
If I could live those days again,
    I'd make Him Lord of all.

Theodore W. Brennan

God's strength behind you, His concern for you, His love within you, and His arms beneath you are more than sufficient for the job ahead of you.

William Arthur Ward

He prayeth best who loveth best
All things both great and small;
For the dear God who loves us,
He made and loveth all.

Samuel Taylor Coleridge

The Christ Of Calvary!

CHRIST does not save men by His life,
    Though that was holy, sinless, pure;
Nor even by His tender love,
    Though that forever shall endure;
He does not save them by His words,
    Though they shall never pass away;
Nor by His vast creative power
    That holds the elements in sway;
He does not save them by His works,
    Though He was ever doing good;
The awful need was greater still,
    It took His death, His cross, His blood.

Men preach today a crossless Christ,
    A strengthless Saviour, vague and dim;
They will not see their sinful state,
    They will not own their need of Him.
They will not know the Lamb of God,
    Despised, rejected, crucified;
That were to humble into dust
    Their boasted intellect, their pride.
Yet no man cometh unto God
    Save by the Son alone, He saith;
The deathless life for which we long
    Can only, ever come through death.

Not Bethlehem, not Nazareth,
    Stern Justice's lifted hand could stay;
To Calvary the soul must go,
    And follow Jesus *all the way.*

Annie Johnson Flint

Might

They had sealed the tomb, they had kept a watch,
The military men of their day,
And yet they were utterly powerless—
The stone was rolled away.

They waited like men who were long dead.
Their jangling swords were stilled,
And there in the garden the Christ arose
That his word might be fulfilled.

As calm as the steadfast stars at night,
As still as the garden close,
The dawn broke over the farthest hills
The morning that Christ arose.

The dawn breaks over our world today.
There is light on the hills once more,
Neither war, nor rumors of war can hold
The stone at the tomb's dark door.

No might at all had the power to bind
The Christ whom they left as dead.
Nations and thrones may fall, but He
Is risen as He said!

Grace Noll Crowell

GOLDEN NUGGETS

"He is not here. He is risen." Upon that great fact hangs the entire plan of the redemptive program of God. Without the resurrection of Christ there could be no salvation, no hope for the future. The resurrection meant that God had accepted his Son's atoning work on the cross: He was "delivered for our offenses, and was raised again for our justification." The sting of death is gone and Christ now holds the keys of death.

We do not leave Christ hanging on a cross with blood streaming down from his hands, his side and his feet. Early on that first Easter morning the angel gave to Mary, Mary Magdalene and Salome the greatest, the most glorious news that human ear has ever heard: "He is not here. He is risen."

Billy Graham

The Mother's Question

When I was a boy, and it chanced to rain,
  Mother would always watch for me;
She used to stand by the window pane,
  Worried and troubled as she could be.
And this was the question I used to hear,
The very minute that I drew near;
The words she used, I can't forget:
"Tell me, my boy, if your feet are wet."

Worried about me was mother dear,
  As healthy a lad as ever strolled
Over a turnpike, far or near,
  'Fraid to death that I'd take a cold.
Always stood by the window pane,
Watching for me in the pouring rain;
And her words in my ears are ringing yet:
"Tell me, my boy, if your feet are wet."

Stockings warmed by the kitchen fire,
  And slippers ready for me to wear;
Seemed that mother would never tire,
  Giving her boy the best of care,
Thinking of him the long day through,
In the worried way that all mothers do;
Whenever it rained she'd start to fret,
Always fearing my feet were wet.

And now, whenever it rains, I see
  A vision of mother in days of yore,
Still waiting there to welcome me,
  As she used to do by the open door.
And always I think as I enter there
Of a mother's love and a mother's care;
Her words in my ears are ringing yet:
"Tell me, my boy, if your feet are wet."

Edgar Guest

Question For The First Day Of School

Time again for erasers and tablets—remember?
Some hearts must skip backward, while young feet
  skip on.
Why is it the loudest footsteps, each September,
Are those of the children who have grown up and gone?

Minni Hite Moody

Today

I have spread wet linen
On lavender bushes,
I have swept rose petals
From a garden walk.
I have labeled jars of raspberry jam,
I have baked a sunshine cake;
I have embroidered a yellow duck
On a small blue frock.
I have polished andirons,
Dusted the highboy,
Cut sweet peas for a black bowl,
Wound the tall clock,
Pleated a lace ruffle . . .
To-day
I have lived a poem.

Ethel Romig Fuller

With This Faith

Home has to be more than the place
    where a man finds his
Safe harbor of retreat from
    the abrasions of the world—

More, even, than the place
    where he discerns the
Personal haven of his spirit.

Home has to be the place where
    a man has a purpose;
    where he belongs;
Where he is loved and needed
    and respected;
Where he has a job to do,
    a cause,
And loyalties that lead him
    to discover
A meaning for his life.

Jerry Lipman

When Comes The Time

Lord of small boys—and Lord of mothers, too,
And Guardian of those years when each scuffed shoe
Still knows the sill of home—so much depends on You.
Here at their inner shrine I still belong
To light the candles and to sing the song
That keeps their courage high, their feet from wrong.

But as the springtime slipped away before
That marked the time a mother led of yore
Her young child, Samuel, to the Temple's door,
These apple-climbing days will fade. For then
I, too, shall stand before a temple when
The winging years have turned my boys to men;

And I, like Hannah, at the threshold wait
Nor am allowed the veil to desecrate . . .
As small hands cling to mine, Lord, recreate
The spark to build of cedar, flame, and steel
The Holy Place where they Your Presence feel;
An altar there—where boys, grown up, can kneel.

Muriel Shrader Mann

To Understand A Child

To understand a child is to begin
A journey through a land of mystery.
To help another being to unfold,
And yet to leave its seeking spirit free.
Impatience is a detour on the path
And loss of temper is a desert place
Where understanding for a while is
   gone
Until there is an honest search for
   grace.
There must be putting of the self aside,
A deep humility that ever waits
To guard and guide, to stop and listen
   well,
A mother love that never hesitates
To show itself no matter what the hour,
That gains its inner strength from God's
   own power.

Louise Darcy

Child And Brook

Today my child has known a brook.
At first she stood with probing toe
Thrust and withdrawn, with intent
Eager but fearful. Then slow
Delight possessed her. The chill
Spray feathered her ankles, the swift
Water sang past her feet; in still
Warm shallows she watched the drift
Of bubbled foam, saw skippers dart.
She stroked the stones, felt ripples play.
Later she'll hold this hour apart
Remembering this brook today.

Elizabeth Anderson

Golden Thoughts

The happiest moments of my life have been the few
which I have passed at home in the bosom of my family.

Thomas Jefferson

Next to God, thy parents.

William Penn

Wonder Lies In A Round Rainbow

That year I was ten. My father was the minister of a small church in a Midwestern town. This was already my third school, and I was in the fifth grade. I hoped we wouldn't have to move again.

One day Celia spoke to me. She was the jeweler's daughter. They lived in a big white house and went to the stone church on their side of town.

"See my diamond ring?" Tossing her long black hair like a restless pony, she stretched out her hand. On her little finger was a thin gold band set with a diamond. Colors flashed, and I saw the sky and the green of leaves reflected in the stone.

"It's only a little one." She tossed her hair again. "Daddy says I can have a big one when I graduate from high school." I couldn't think of anything to say. Celia laughed and walked away with two of her friends.

One day after school I told my father, "I don't have any friends." I knew I was going to cry and before I knew what I was saying, I sobbed, "Celia has a diamond ring." He was sitting at the desk in his big, high-backed chair. "Come, Caryl." He motioned to the chair across from him. "Come, let us read together."

He handed me a volume of German poetry. I took the heavy brown book. It smelled of old leather and its thin pages made soft whispering sounds as I turned them. Through my tears I began to read aloud.

"That is good, Caryl," my father said, "but turn the *r* more on your tongue. Like a bird's note."

All the while my father and I read, I knew he was seeing, from some window of his memory, towers on the Rhine, the flowing river; breathing the golden air of his homeland. I looked at the rows of books on the walls, thinking that my father knew everything in all of them. I wondered whether someday I would acquire all knowledge available to mankind as he had done.

That year my mother and I wore clothes that came in missionary boxes. Mother did not enjoy sewing, but she altered the clothes so we could wear them. She cut down a gray coat for me. It was the right length when she finished, but it was broad in the shoulders and roomy in the sleeves. She pinned a red flower on the lapel.

The dresses I wore to school were sometimes crepe or satin. I knew I was different. The other girls knew it, too. But in the evenings my father would wind up the old phonograph and put on a record. He would smile at my mother and me and say, "Now. Mozart." Then everything was all right, and we were safe there together with the music, with one another.

One spring day the girls were talking about Celia's birthday party. "Remember the clown last year?" one girl said. "I love circus parties!"

"I liked the one before that when they took us all to the movies," said another girl. "What is it going to be this year, Celia?"

Celia laughed. "It's a secret," she said, looking at us as we stood there in a ring around her. "It's going to be the best one of all. I'm sending the invitations in the mail. Everybody's invitation will come in the mail."

I told my mother about it. I told her I wished I could have a new dress for the party. A real dress. A dress of my own. "What can I give Celia?" I asked my mother. What can you give a girl who has a diamond ring?

I did not get a new dress. Not really. Mother cut down a white cotton and I felt almost right in it. She made an apron and helped me embroider Celia on the pocket in little blue letters. I thought it was beautiful.

At school the girls talked about the invitations they had received. I heard them talking to each other, but they would change the subject when I came near. I had a sick feeling that Celia was not going to ask me, that I would be the only one not going to her party.

But she seemed friendly to me. She said, "Caryl, I wish I could write a poem like the one you wrote. The one Miss Jameson read in class yesterday."

I hoped again. If she liked my poem, maybe she liked me, too. Three days before the party I called to my mother when I came home from school. "Mother, has my invitation come yet?"

Father answered. "Your mother is not at home, *Liebchen*. There was no mail." As he looked at me, he seemed to know what I was thinking. "Do this for me, please," he said. "I have not yet seen the new dress. Put it on, that I may see how you look in it."

I went to my room and put on the white dress. I combed my straight hair and stared at myself, solemn and pale in the shadowy mirror. Then I went downstairs and stood before my father.

"Turn around." I revolved before him slowly. "Like a flower," he said. "Like a snowdrop. But are those the shoes to wear with such a dress?" I wore my brown oxfords. "Come," he said, "come." Together we went down into the town.

When my mother came home, I heard them talking, but I couldn't hear all they said. I was in my room with my new shoes. I had never had black patent-leather slippers before. I stroked the surface of them, mirror bright. I smelled the fresh new smell of them. I felt them smooth and strong against the skin of my fingers, and then, princesslike on my feet. For my father I would have walked on swords, like the little mermaid. But in my new shoes there were only shafts of love.

On the day of the party my invitation still had not come. That Saturday afternoon was balmy with spring. I put on my white dress and my new shoes and sat on the back porch to wait for the mailman. Celia's package was beside me. My mother came out and stood by me.

"Do you suppose I will ever have a diamond ring?" I asked her. I took her hand, the one with the ring on it, and looked into the diamond. It was smaller than Celia's and I could not see the myriad colors I had seen in Celia's ring; only a hint of red, a shadow of blue.

Then I saw Mr. Elliot, the mailman, walk past the corner. I went into the house and watched from the hall window. He didn't even pause. He walked right by our mailbox. And then I knew for sure.

I went up to my room and shut the door. Tearing the wrapping off Celia's apron, I crumpled it into a ball and threw it on the floor. I took off my white dress and put on my Saturday clothes. I started to take off my new shoes, but

Continued on Page 44

Continued from Page 43

then the tears came. I lay on my bed with my face in the pillow and I cried for a long time. My throat hurt and it was hard to breathe. After a while, though, the tears stopped. I smoothed out the apron, washed my face, and went down to the back porch again.

Soon my father came out and placed a bowl of soapy water beside me. He laid a piece of an old woolen mitten on the step. I had worn those mittens the year I was four. Mother had knit them. Then he put a wooden bubble pipe on my lap. I looked at it and held it against my face. The wood was smooth and tan, and it touched me comfortably, like my father's hand.

I dipped into the soapsuds and blew a family of small bubbles which flew away on the soft wind. The bubble pipe tasted woody and tart, faintly tinged with soap.

Holding the woolen mitten on my left hand, I began to blow a large bubble. Evenly letting out my breath in tiny wisps of air, I watched it grow. There were little windows in it. When it was ripe, I flicked it carefully from the bowl of my pipe to the piece of wool and held it while it quivered and shimmered. There would never again be one just like it. I made it myself, and when it left me it would go where all bubbles go.

As I looked at it, just before it burst, I saw the most lovely colors. I saw the sky and the budding trees. I saw the back door of my house, and although I did not see my parents, I knew they were there. I saw all the fragile wonders of the world. And when at last my bubble burst, I felt the cool and gentle moisture on my cheek.

Caryl Porter

Especially For You

"I made it 'specially for you,"
    He said, and handed me
The dubious daub of color
    He had made for me to see.

A horse? A cat? A fish? A shoe?
    Who quibbles with such art?
No matter what it was I knew
    It came straight from his heart.

I told him it was beautiful—
    I loved his big surprise!
And a million dollars couldn't buy
    That pleased look in his eyes.

"Especially for you"—three words
    Such potent magic hold.
They turn the smallest gift on earth
    To one of purest gold.

Helen Lowrie Marshall

The Children's Hour

Between the dark and the daylight,
  When the night is beginning to lower,
Comes a pause in the day's occupations,
  That is known as the Children's Hour.

I hear in the chamber above me
  The patter of little feet,
The sound of a door that is opened
  And voices soft and sweet.

From my study I see in the lamplight,
  Descending the broad hall stair,
Grave Alice, and laughing Allegra
  And Edith with golden hair.

A whisper, and then a silence:
  Yet I know by their merry eyes
They are plotting and planning together
  To take me by surprise.

A sudden rush from the stairway,
  A sudden raid from the hall!
By three doors left unguarded
  They enter my castle wall!

Do you think, O blue-eyed banditti,
  Because you have scaled the wall,
Such an old moustache as I am
  Is not a match for you all!

I have you fast in my fortress,
  And will not let you depart,
But put you down into the dungeon
  In the round-tower of my heart.

And there will I keep you forever,
  Yes, forever and a day,
Till the wall shall crumble to ruin,
  And moulder in dust away!

Henry Wadsworth Longfellow

The Freedom Of Love

Repeatedly, I have written of the creative liberty I have been given in my own life through the freeing love offered me for all my years by my mother. By my father too, when he was alive. I must have often perplexed them both during the years in which I was not a Christian. But always, their love came toward me, reminding me of their faith in me, of their generosity, of their expectations for me. I was never permitted to stop believing in myself. To this day, I am convinced that their love, the quality of their love, ultimately did this for me. My own belief in myself bent often and broke once or twice. Theirs never wavered. As with every family, mine had its share of good times and bad times. Not once, through either, did they try to force their problems upon me by insisting (as they had every right to do because they supported me much of the time) that I "come home" in order to make things easier for them for one reason or another. They believed in me and believed that I would make my goal of becoming a professional writer more quickly in a big city, so through any vicissitude of theirs, I was left free.

The results in my life were slow to appear. I still marvel at their patience. But one example of how their unselfish, freeing love got through to me at perhaps the most self-centered period of my life shows the creative effect of their love on me in a rather concrete way. It may sound unimpressive. It may seem what any ordinarily considerate daughter would have done anyway. Not this one. At a time when my career was just beginning to focus my mother fell ill and required serious surgery. It was putting definite financial pressure upon them to keep me in Chicago in my own apartment. Mother needed me with her. My father needed me with him. But they did not intimate even by so much as a look that they expected me to do anything but go on living in the big city "on them." Result? Of my own accord, not because I thought I *had* to, but with all my heart because I *wanted* to, I went home to stay out the year. I was nineteen, and although I didn't do anything else noticeably unselfish until I became a follower of Jesus Christ at the age of thirty-three, I began to like myself a little once I stopped pushing aside obstacles and people in order to protect myself.

The quality of the love I have always received from Mother and Dad conditioned me for quick, rather natural belief in the love of God. They had made it utterly possible for me to believe that God loved me. I admit to some problems with accepting his discipline, but never his love. My parents were, like yours, not perfect. I'm sure I needed more discipline at their hands. But human love at its very highest will always make mistakes in its actions. It is the *reaction* of love that counts.

My parents have loved me freely and in the process conditioned me to love. Even at the first moment of conscious faith in God, I felt at home. I had grown up in the very atmosphere of giving love. Love that left me free to seek my own fulfillment. Love that did not choke my particular personality. Love that did not bend me to the image of anyone. Love that never put me in competition with my brother, nor my brother with me.

Eugenia Price

golden Nuggets

We thank Thee for the hopes that rise
Within her heart, as, day by day,
The dawning soul, from those young eyes,
Looks with a clearer, steadier ray.

William Cullen Bryant

Womanhood

Blessed is the woman who has a smile in her voice, a sparkle in her eyes, a song on her lips, a spring in her step, a warmth in her touch, a depth to her beauty, a purpose to her life, a joy in her faith, a hope in her breast, and a love in her heart.

William Arthur Ward

I Have Found Such Joy

I have found such joy in simple things;
  A plain, clean room, a nut-brown loaf of bread,
A cup of milk, a kettle as it sings,
  The shelter of a roof above my head,
And in a leaf-laced square along the floor,
Where yellow sunlight glimmers through a door.

I have found such joy in things that fill
  My quiet days: a curtain's blowing grace,
A potted plant upon my window sill,
  A rose, fresh-cut and placed within a vase;
A table cleared, a lamp beside a chair,
And books I long have loved beside me there.

Oh, I have found such joys I wish I might
  Tell every woman who goes seeking far
For some elusive, feverish delight,
  That very close to home the great joys are:
The elemental things—old as the race,
Yet never, through the ages, commonplace.

Grace Noll Crowell

GOldEN pRAYERS

We thank Thee. Lord, for happy hearts,
For rain and sunny weather.
We thank Thee, Lord, for this our food,
And that we are together.

Emilie Fendall Johnson

Philosophy For Mothers

When he grows up, I don't think he'll recall
How, on a sapphire morning in the fall,
Dust pussies tumbled up and down the stair,
And smudges lined the woodwork here and there,
While he and I ran hand in hand together,
Carefree, into the bright October weather.

I hope my son looks back upon today
And sees a mother who had time to play
Whether the work was done, or it was not;
Who realized chores are sometimes best forgot.
There will be years for cleaning house and cooking,
But little boys grow up when we're not looking.

Barbara Overton Christie

Ghost House

There's an empty lot on the avenue,
With shady trees and a wrought iron fence,
Once long ago there was a house,
But nobody else has built there since!
I pass that way when I go for walks,
I don't know why but I always do,
And I close my eyes imagining,
How it used to look when it was new.
If I try real hard I can see the roof,
With its stately gables rising high,
Its grey stone walls and a rambling porch,
And wicker chairs on the lawn nearby.
And I sense a warm and friendly air,
... About the house that isn't there!

Grace E. Easley

LET'S READ IT TOGETHER

A Morning Prayer

Through the night Thine angels kept
Watch around me while I slept.
Now the dark has gone away,
Lord, I thank Thee for the day.

Anonymous

Song

I once had a sweet little doll, dears,
    The prettiest doll in the world;
Her cheeks were so red and so white, dears,
    And her hair was so charmingly curled.
But I lost my poor little doll, dears,
    As I played in the heath one day;
And I cried for her more than a week, dears,
    But I never could find where she lay.

I found my poor little doll, dears,
    As I played in the heath one day;
Folks say she is terribly changed, dears,
    For her paint is all washed away,
And her arm trodden off by the cows, dears,
    And her hair not the least bit curled:
Yet for old sakes' sake she is still, dears,
    The prettiest doll in the world.

Charles Kingsley

49

Mary And Her Lamb

Mary had a little lamb,
Its fleece was white as snow,
And everywhere that Mary went
The lamb was sure to go;
He followed her to school one day—
That was against the rule.
It made the children laugh and play
To see a lamb at school.

And so the teacher turned him out,
But still he lingered near,
And waited patiently about
Till Mary did appear;
And then he ran to her, and laid
His head upon her arm,
As if he said, "I'm not afraid—
You'll keep me from all harm."

"What makes the lamb love Mary so?"
The eager children cry.
"Oh, Mary loves the lamb, you know,"
The teacher did reply;
"And you each gentle animal
In confidence may bind
And make them follow at your call,
If you are always kind."

Sarah Josepha Hale

Prayer For Children Everywhere

I have so much—my books and toys,
My home and all those in it,
My food, my happy life, my friends—
I'm thankful every minute!

I want to share my blessings, God,
With all those many others—
Poor children hungry, sick, and cold:
My sisters and my brothers.

Corinna Marsh

A Birthday Grace

God made the sun
    And God made the tree,
God made the mountains
    And God made me.

I thank You, O God.
    For the sun and the tree,
For making the mountains
    And for making me.

Leah Gale

Grace Before Meals

Come, dear Lord Jesus, be our guest, and bless what
Thou hast given us. For Jesus' sake. Amen.

From the German

Cradle Hymn

Away in a manger, no crib for a bed,
The little Lord Jesus laid down his sweet head.
The stars in the bright sky looked down where he lay—
The little Lord Jesus asleep on the hay.

The cattle are lowing, the baby awakes,
But little Lord Jesus no crying he makes.
I love Thee, Lord Jesus! Look down from the sky,
And stay by my cradle till morning is nigh.

Be near me, Lord Jesus, I ask Thee to stay
Close by me forever, and love me, I pray.
Bless all the dear children, in Thy tender care,
And take us to heaven, to live with Thee there.

Martin Luther

Gentle Jesus

Gentle Jesus, meek and mild,
Look upon a little child!

Make me gentle as Thou art,
Come and live within my heart.

Take my childish hand in Thine,
Guide these little feet of mine.

So shall all my happy days
Sing their pleasant song of praise;

And the world shall always see
Christ, the Holy Child, in me.

Charles Wesley

A Child's Thanksgiving Prayer

I thank Thee God: for stars and sun
for friends and fun
for Mom and Dad
for blessings had
for soil and seeds
for His loving deeds
for joys in living
for good in giving
for my church and school
and wisdom to live by the Golden Rule

Dian Kilby

Jesus, Friend of little children,
Be a Friend to me;
Take my hand and ever keep me
Close to Thee.

Walter J. Mathans

Daily Life

Adverbs

May I seek to live this day
    quietly, easily,
leaning on Your mighty strength
    trustfully, restfully,
meeting others in the path
    peacefully, joyously,
waiting for Your will's unfolding
    patiently, serenely,
facing what tomorrow brings
    confidently, courageously.

Author Unknown

I Wish You

I wish you
some new love
of lovely things,
and some new forgetfulness
of the teasing things,
and some higher pride
in the praising things,
and some sweeter peace
from the hurrying things,
and some closer fence
from the worrying things.

John Ruskin

Golden Thoughts

I walk with God daily.

Helen Keller

Commit Thy Way Unto The Lord

Commit thy way unto the Lord
And trust in His unchanging Word;
He'll guide thee safely all the way
And guard and keep thee night and day.

What if thy path be rough and steep
And sorrow cause thine eyes to weep,
Thy Savior knows thy bitter cup
And His strong arm will hold thee up.

What if thy children go astray
And walk not in the narrow way—
Commit them all to Jesus' care—
Then pray—and love—and leave them there.

What if thy wealth be swept away,
Thy home bereft in one short day—
In paths like these men oft have trod,
And found they led them home to God.

Howard W. Pope

GOLDEN THOUGHTS

Yourself in your own hands is a problem and a pain;
yourself in the hands of God is a possibility and a power.

E. Stanley Jones

I never did anything worth doing by accident, nor
did any of my inventions come by accident; they came
by work.

Thomas Edison

A Morning Hymn

Christ, whose glory fills the skies,
   Christ, the true, the only Light,
Sun of Righteousness, arise,
   Triumph o'er the shades of night:
Dayspring from on high, be near;
Daystar, in my heart appear.

Dark and cheerless is the morn,
   Unaccompanied by Thee;
Joyless is the day's return,
   Till Thy mercy's beams I see;
Till Thy inward light impart,
Glad my eyes, and warm my heart.

Visit then this soul of mine;
   Pierce the gloom of sin and grief;
Fill me, Radiancy divine;
   Scatter all my unbelief:
More and more Thyself display,
Shining to the perfect Day.

Charles Wesley

Dear Lord, I offer thee this day
All I shall think, or do, or say.

Author Unknown

From me is thy fruit found.

Hosea 14:8

A Little Human Happiness

"I never met a man I didn't like," said Will Rogers, and probably the reason the great American cowboy-humorist could make that statement was that few, if any, were the men who did not like Will Rogers. An incident that happened when Rogers was a young cowboy in Oklahoma helps explain it.

In the winter of 1898, Rogers fell heir to a ranch near Claremore. One day a farmer who lived nearby killed one of Will's steers that had broken down a fence and eaten his young corn. According to range custom, the farmer should have informed Will what he had done and why. He did not do so, and when Rogers found out about it, he was fit to be tied. Flaming with wrath, he called a hired hand to accompany him and rode forth to have it out with the farmer.

During the ride, a blue norther struck, coating the cowboys and their horses with ice. When they arrived at the farmer's cabin, he wasn't home. But the farmer's wife insisted that the frozen men come in and wait by the fire for his return. While warming himself, Rogers noticed how thin and workworn the woman was. He also noticed five scrawny children peeking at him from behind various pieces of furniture.

When the farmer returned, his wife told him how Rogers and his companion had ridden out of the storm. Will started to light into the man, then suddenly closed his mouth and offered his hand instead. The farmer, unaware of the reason for Will's visit, accepted the proffered hand and invited them to stay for supper. "You'll have to eat beans," he apologized, "for the storm has interrupted the butchering of my steer."

The two visitors accepted the invitation.

All during the meal Rogers' companion kept waiting for Will to say something about the slaughtered steer; but Rogers just continued to laugh and joke with the family, and watch as the children's eyes lighted up every time they mentioned the beef they would eat on the morrow and during the weeks to come.

The norther was still blowing when supper was finished, so the farmer and his wife insisted that the two men stay the night. They did.

The next morning they were sent on their way with a bellyful of black coffee and hot beans and biscuits. Still, Rogers had not mentioned the reason for his visit. As they rode away, Will's companion began to chide him. "I thought you were going to lay that sodbuster low about your steer," he said.

Will remained silent for a few moments, then replied, "I intended to, but then I got to thinking. You know, I really didn't lose that steer. I just traded it for a little human happiness. There are millions of steers in the world, but human happiness is kinda scarce."

Albert P. Hout

🐿🐿🐿🐿🐿

Good temper, like a sunny day, sheds a brightness over everything. It is the sweetness of toil and the soother of disquietude.

Washington Irving

My Day

This be my day—
Some honest work,
A bit of play—
To laugh and love,
And live and pray
With God beside me
All the way—
This be my day.

Helen Lowrie Marshall

Partners With God

Whatever tasks we find to do,
Whatever projects we pursue,
    Whatever path we plod,
It is a cheering thought that we
In all our daily toil may be
    In partnership with God!
For not alone by pastures green,
Nor where the brooklet flows serene
    Does He bestow His care;
But in the crowded marts as well,
Where men may bargain, buy, and sell,
    He'll walk beside us there.

Clarence Mansfield Lindsay

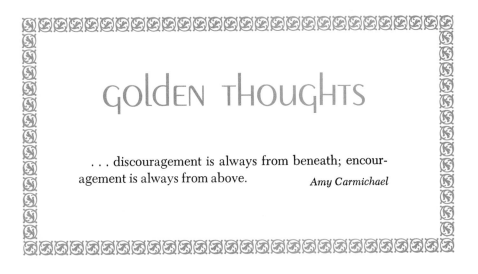

GOLDEN THOUGHTS

. . . discouragement is always from beneath; encouragement is always from above.
Amy Carmichael

Half the joy of life is in little things taken on the run. Let us run if we must—even the sands do that—but let us keep our hearts young and our eyes open that nothing worth our while shall escape us.

Victor Cherbuliez

Beauty

Beauty is seen
In the sunlight,
The trees, the birds,
Corn growing and people working
Or dancing for their harvest.
Beauty is heard
In the night,
Wind sighing, rain falling,
Or a singer chanting
Anything in earnest.
Beauty is in yourself.
Good deeds, happy thoughts
That repeat themselves
In your dreams,
In your work,
And even in your rest.

E-Yeh-Shure

Example

Like the star
Shining afar
Slowly now
And without rest,
Let each man turn, with steady sway,
Round the task that rules the day
And do his best.

Johann Wolfgang Von Goethe

GOLDEN NUGGETS

God uses broken things. It takes broken soil to produce a crop, broken clouds to give rain, broken grain to give bread, broken bread to give strength. It is the broken alabaster box that gives forth perfume. . . . It is Peter, weeping bitterly, who returns to greater power than ever.

Vance Havner

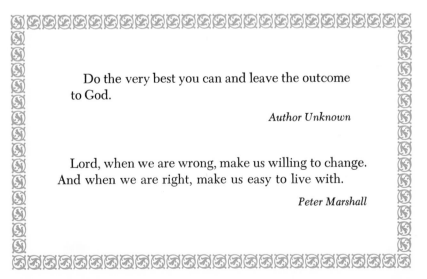

Do the very best you can and leave the outcome to God.

Author Unknown

Lord, when we are wrong, make us willing to change. And when we are right, make us easy to live with.

Peter Marshall

The Whistle

When I was a child of seven years old, my friends on a holiday filled my little pocket with hapence. I went directly to a shop where they sold toys for children; and being charmed with the sound of a whistle that I met by the way, in the hands of another boy, I voluntarily offered and gave all my money for it. When I came home, whistling all over the house, much pleased with my whistle, but disturbing all the family; my brothers, sisters, and cousins, understanding the bargain I had made, told me I had given four times as much for it as it was worth; put me in mind what good things I might have bought with the rest of the money; and laughed at me so much for my folly, that I cried with vexation; and the reflection gave me more chagrin than the whistle gave me pleasure.

This however was afterwards of use to me, the impression continuing on my mind;.so that often, when I was tempted to buy some unnecessary thing, I said to myself, "Do not give too much for the whistle"; and I saved my money.

Benjamin Franklin

In this big wide world of ours,
God has made enough sunshine
For everyone to have a share,
Sometime . . . Somewhere.

Zelda Davis Howard

May this morning light illumine
our day and purify our souls.
Let our tongues form no devious words;
let our minds harbour no dark thoughts.

Aurelius Clemens

How Do You Tackle Your Work?

How do you tackle your work each day?
    Are you scared of the job you find?
Do you grapple the task that comes your way
    With a confident, easy mind?
Do you stand right up to the work ahead
    Or fearfully pause to view it?
Do you start to toil with a sense of dread
    Or feel that you're going to do it?

You can do as much as you think you can,
    But you'll never accomplish more;
If you're afraid of yourself, young man,
    There's little for you in store.
For failure comes from the inside first,
    It's there if we only knew it,
And you can win, though you face the worst,
    If you feel that you're going to do it.

Success! It's found in the soul of you,
    And not in the realm of luck!
The world will furnish the work to do,
    But you must provide the pluck.
You can do whatever you think you can,
    It's all in the way you view it.
It's all in the start that you make, young man:
    You must feel that you're going to do it.

How do you tackle your work each day?
    With confidence clear, or dread?
What to yourself do you stop and say
    When a new task lies ahead?
What is the thought that is in your mind?
    Is fear ever running through it?
If so, tackle the next you find
    By thinking you're going to do it.

Edgar Guest

Today, O Lord

O Lord, I pray
That for this day
   I may not swerve
By foot or hand
From Thy command
   Not to be served, but to serve.

This, too, I pray,
That from this day
   No love of ease
Nor pride prevent
My good intent
   Not to be pleased, but to please.

And if I may
I'd have this day
   Strength from above
To set my heart
In heavenly art
   Not to be loved, but to love.

Maltbie D. Babcock

The Happy Man

If you observe a really happy man you will find him building a boat, writing a symphony, educating his son, growing double dahlias in his garden, or looking for dinosaur eggs in the Gobi desert. He will not be searching for happiness as if it were a collar button that has rolled under the radiator. He will not be striving for it as if it were a goal in itself, nor will he be seeking for it among the nebulous wastes of metaphysics.

To find happiness we must seek for it in a focus outside ourselves.

W. Beran Wolfe

The freshness of that morning hour
I felt the whole day through;
The presence of his mighty pow'r
Made tasks so light to do.
The way was fragrant with his love
Till bitter things grew sweet,
Till I rejoiced to wait his move
And linger near his feet.

Alice Reynolds Flower

Greet the dawn with enthusiasm and you may
expect satisfaction at sunset.

Author Unknown

Today

Build a little fence of trust
Around today;
Fill the space with loving deeds,
And therein stay.
Look not through the sheltering bars
Upon tomorrow;
God will help thee bear what comes
Of joy or sorrow.

Mary Frances Butts

Gentleness

Gentle the seedling breaks through chilly soil.
A gentle hand removes the weeds around it.
Gently spent leaves fall in their time
And softly cover.

There is enough cruel in rains and winds,
Sun and cold: no poisons needed.
God uses human hands to spread
Gentleness on earth.
Ellen Young

Keep your face to the sunshine and you cannot see
the shadow.
Helen Keller

Labour to keep alive in your breast that little spark
of celestial fire,—conscience.
George Washington

Keep conscience clear, then never fear.
Benjamin Franklin

Fragrance is like light. It cannot be hidden. It is like love: intangible, invisible, but always at once recognized. Though it is neither to be touched, nor heard, nor seen, we know that it is there. And its opposite is just as impossible to hide. This brings us to a solemn truth: it is what we *are* that tells.[1]

Amy Carmichael

If you insist on perfection, make the first demand on yourself.

Author Unknown

Prayer At Dawn

When morning breaks and I face the day,
This, dear Lord, is what I pray.
That when the same day fades to gray,
Some child of yours may happier be,
May find himself more close to Thee,
Because I lived this day.

Jule Creaser

Living By Grace

Grace is doing for another being kindnesses he doesn't deserve, hasn't earned, could not ask for, and can't repay. Its main facets are beauty, kindness, gratitude, charm, favor, and thankfulness. Grace offers man what he cannot do for himself. The unwritten creed of many is that God is under obligation to them, but grace suggests that we are under obligation to God. To live in that consciousness is to live by grace. Living by grace is costly; it means sharing. It has no meaning apart from a spirit of self-sacrifice that prompts the soul to think more of giving than of receiving, of caring for others rather than for one's self.

Paul McElroy

No frown ever made a heart glad; no complaint ever made a dark day bright; no bitter word ever lightened a burden or made a rough road smooth; no grumbling ever made the sun shine in a home. The day needs the resolute step, the look of cheer, the smiling countenance, the kindly word.

Unknown

It is easier to supress the first desire than to satisfy all that follow it.

Benjamin Franklin

We live in this world, that is true. But the point of living is: don't be subdued by it.

Billy Graham

Simile

Truth is love—
bright as sunlight
clear as living water
soft as moonlight
old as time
sure as eternity.

Clyta Shaw

🦋🦋🦋🦋🦋🦋🦋🦋🦋🦋🦋🦋🦋🦋🦋🦋🦋🦋🦋

Nature gives to every time and season some beauties of its own.

Charles Dickens

🦋🦋🦋🦋🦋🦋🦋🦋🦋🦋🦋🦋🦋🦋🦋🦋🦋🦋🦋

Courtesy

Courtesy is a quality of soul refinement impossible to purchase, impossible to acquire at easy cost.

Politeness is but the shallow imitation of courtesy, and often masquerades as a refining quality in life when it is courtesy that truly refines mankind. Politeness can be assumed, courtesy never. One can be trained upon the surface of the mind, the other must be born in the soul.

Noble natures are often impolite, often lack surface politeness, but have real courtesy in the soul, where great and good men really live. They would not, they could not stoop to low cunning or contemptible meanness.

Polite people may be the very quintessence of cunning, so artful that the world regards them as delightful people until their shallow souls are uncovered. The difference between the polite person and the courteous soul is as wide as the gulf that separates evil from good.

F. E. Elwell

golden prayers

Almighty God, whose light is of Eternity and knoweth no setting, shine forth and be our safeguard through the night; and though the earth be wrapped in darkness and the heavens be veiled from our sight, let Thy brightness be about our beds, and Thy peace within our souls, and Thy Fatherly blessing upon our sleep this night.

Amen.

Author Unknown

Now The Day Is Over

Now the day is over,
Night is drawing nigh,
Shadows of the evening
Steal across the sky;

Jesus, give the weary
Calm and sweet repose;
With Thy tenderest blessing
May our eyelids close.

Grant to little children
Visions bright of thee;
Guard the sailors tossing
On the deep blue sea.

Comfort every sufferer
Watching late in pain;
Those who plan some evil
From their sins restrain.

Through the long night watches,
May Thine angels spread
Their white wings above me,
Watching round my bed.

When the morning wakens,
Then may I arise
Pure and fresh and sinless
In Thy holy eyes.

Sabine Baring-Gould

American Heritage

Speak Gently

Speak gently! It is better far
    To rule by love than fear;
Speak gently; let no harsh words mar
    The good we might do here!

Speak gently! Love doth whisper low
    The vow that true hearts bind;
And gently Friendship's accents flow;
    Affection's voice is kind.

Speak gently to the little child!
    Its love be sure to gain;
Teach it in accents soft and mild;
    It may not long remain.

Speak gently to the young, for they
    Will have enough to bear;
Pass through this life as best they may,
    'Tis full of anxious care!

Speak gently to the aged one,
    Grieve not the care-worn heart;
Whose sands of life are nearly run,
    Let such in peace depart!

Speak gently, kindly, to the poor;
    Let no harsh tone be heard;
They have enough they must endure,
    Without an unkind word!

Speak gently to the erring; know
    They may have toiled in vain;
Perchance unkindness made them so:
    Oh, win them back again!

David Bates

GOLDEN THOUGHTS

The God who gave us life, gave us liberty at the same time.

Thomas Jefferson

Whatever makes men good Christians, makes them good citizens.

Daniel Webster

I believe that every right implies a responsibility; every opportunity, an obligation; every possession, a duty.

John D. Rockefeller, Jr.

I Love America

I love America, where truth can be shouted from the housetops, instead of whispered in dismal cellars hidden from the spies and dictators.

I love America, where families can sleep peacefully without fear of secret seizure and torture in some foul prison, or purged in blood for political reasons.

I love America, where men are truly free men; not living in fear of slavery, exile, or involuntary servitude, while their homes are confiscated and loved ones are turned weeping and sorrowing from their doors.

I love America, where there are equal rights for all, and where people are not forced to hate, persecute, or kill because of religion, race, or creed.

I love America, where little children are not forced to suffer for want of bread withheld at the whim of some despot carrying out a plan for greater glory.

I love America, where men can think as they please, and where thought is not regulated by decrees, enforced with bullets and bayonets.

I love America, where there is love, laughter, hope, and opportunity, and not hate, sorrow, dejection, and futility.

I love America, despite her present troubles because free men can cure them.

I love America, and I will gladly give my life to preserve the freedom our forefathers created, so that our children and their descendants can forever enjoy blessings we have inherited.

Franklin E. Jordan

Lift Every Voice And Sing

Lift every voice and sing, till earth and
    heaven ring,
Ring with the harmonies of liberty;
Let our rejoicing rise, high as the
    list'ning skies,
Let it resound loud as the rolling sea.

Sing a song full of the faith that the dark
    past has taught us.
Sing a song full of the hope that the present
    has brought us;
Facing the rising sun of our newly day begun,
Let us march on till victory is won.

Stony the road we trod, bitter the
    chastening rod,
Felt in the days when hope unborn had died;
Yet with a steady beat, have not our weary
    feet
Come to the place for which our fathers
    sighed?

We have come over a way that with tears has
    been watered;
We have come, treading our path through
    the flood of the slaughtered;
Out from the gloomy past, 'til now we
    stand at last
Where the white gleam of our bright star
    is cast.

God of our weary years, God of our
    silent tears.
Thou who hast brought us thus far on
    the way;
Thou who hast by thy might led us into
    the light,
Keep us forever in thy path, we pray.
Lest our feet stray from the places, our
    God, where we met thee,
Lest, our hearts, drunk with the wine of the
    world, we forget thee;
Shadowed beneath thy hand, may we forever
    stand,
True to our God, true to our native land.

James Weldon Johnson

Columbus

Behind him lay the gray Azores,
    Behind the Gates of Hercules;
Before him not the ghost of shores,
    Before him only shoreless seas.
The good mate said: "Now must we pray,
    For lo! the very stars are gone.
Brave Admiral, speak, what shall I say?"
    "Why, say, 'Sail on! sail on! and on!' "

"My men grow mutinous day by day;
    My men grow ghastly wan and weak."
The stout mate thought of home: a spray
    Of salt wave washed his swarthy cheek.
"What shall I say, brave Admiral, say,
    If we sight naught but seas at dawn?"
"Why, you shall say at break of day,
    'Sail on! sail on! sail on! and on!' "

They sailed and sailed, as winds might blow,
    Until at last the blanched mate said:
"Why, now not even God would know
    Should I and all my men fall dead.
These very winds forget their way,
    For God from these dread seas is gone.
Now speak, brave Admiral, speak and say"—
    He said: "Sail on! sail on! and on!"

They sailed. They sailed. Then spake the mate:
    "This mad sea shows his teeth tonight.
He curls his lip, he lies in wait,
    With lifted teeth as if to bite!
Brave Admiral, say but one good word:
    What shall we do when hope is gone?"
The words leapt like a leaping sword:
    "Sail on! sail on! sail on! and on!"

Joaquin Miller

Our union is now complete; our constitution composed, established and approved. You are now the guardians of your own liberties.

Samuel Adams

Man On His Knees

In the early days of the Republic, a stranger once asked at Congress how he could distinguish Washington.

He was told, "You can easily distinguish him when Congress goes to prayer. Washington is the gentleman who kneels."

Anonymous

Thou Passest Through

"When thou passest through the waters"
   Deep the waves may be and cold,
But Jehovah is our refuge,
   And His promise is our hold;
For the Lord Himself hath said it,
   He, the faithful God and true:
"When thou comest to the waters
   Thou shalt not go down, but through."

Seas of sorrow, seas of trial,
   Bitterest anguish, fiercest pain,
Rolling surges of temptation
   Sweeping over heart and brain—
They shall never overflow us
   For we know His Word is true;
All His waves and all His billows
   He will lead us safely through.

Threatening breakers of destruction,
   Doubts insidious undertow,
Shall not sink us, shall not drag us
   Out to ocean depths of woe;
For His promise shall sustain us,
   Praise the Lord, whose Word is true!
We shall not go down, or under,
   For He saith, "Thou passest through."

Annie Johnson Flint

GOLDEN NUGGETS

I have now disposed of all my property to my family. There is one thing more I wish I could give them, and that is the Christian religion. If they had that, and I had not given them one shilling, they would have been rich, and if they had not that, and I had given them all the world, they would be poor.

Patrick Henry

A Faith To Live By

Give me the faith of adventure, Lord,
  The courage to try the new,
The will to press on in spite of the dark,
  Knowing I walk with You.

Give me the faith of desire and hope,
  The inward urge to achieve.
All things are possible with You.
  O Lord, let me believe!

Give me the faith of awareness
  Of beauty everywhere,
Eyes to see, and ears to hear—
  An open heart to care.

Give me a faith to *live* by,
  Joyous and unafraid,
A glorious faith to match the dawn
  Of this day You have made!

Helen Lowrie Marshall

Look well to the hearthstone; there all hope for America lies.

Calvin Coolidge

Woodman, Spare That Tree!

Woodman, spare that tree!
Touch not a single bough!
In youth it shelter'd me,
And I'll protect it now.
'Twas my forefather's hand
That placed it near his cot;
There, woodman, let it stand,
Thy axe shall harm it not!

That old familiar tree,
Whose glory and renown
Are spread o'er land and sea—
And wouldst thou hew it down?
Woodman, forbear thy stroke!
Cut not its earth-bound ties;
Oh, spare that aged Oak
Now tow'ring to the skies!

When but an idle boy,
I sought its grateful shade;
In all their gushing joy
Here, too, my sisters play'd.
My Mother kiss'd me here;
My Father press'd my hand—
Forgive this foolish tear:
But let that old Oak stand!

My heart-strings round thee cling
Close as thy bark, old friend!
There shall the wild-bird sing,
And still thy branches bend.
Old tree! the storm still brave!
Then, woodman, leave the spot;
While I've a hand to save,
Thy axe shall harm it not.

G. P. Morris

79

Brumidi: "Artist And Citizen Of The U.S.A."

The slender, small-boned man with a military bearing who applied for a job as an artist in Washington, D.C., in 1855 was one of the most promising artists in Italy, well qualified to decorate the unfinished Capitol Building.

"I am Constantine Brumidi and come from Italy three years ago," he announced in broken English. "Am fifty years old and graduate of Academy of Fine Arts in Rome. I help make Capitol Building most beautiful in whole world!"

Brumidi was hired, and when he was informed that as an artist he would receive eight dollars a day, he broke into tears for such wages were unheard of in Europe.

Eager to use his talent on behalf of his adopted land, Brumidi worked furiously. His fellow workers considered the little Italian artist a bit odd. During his lunch hour he would read books on American history. At any parade Brumidi would salute the American flag and tears would come into his eyes.

"Only in this great nation is justice for man like me," he would tell his fellow workers.

It was learned that Brumidi was indeed a great artist in Rome, and up until 1848, a captain of Italian National Guard. In June of 1848, Brumidi was called to duty during the revolution in Rome. Troops patrolled the streets while bands of angry citizens roamed the city setting fires.

A colonel ordered Brumidi to have his men fire upon a group of citizens. The crowd consisted of men and women and several small children. Captain Brumidi shook his head.

"I cannot give that order, sir," he said to the Colonel.

Brumidi was promptly arrested and jailed. In a military prison until 1852, Brumidi was given a choice. He could remain in the prison or leave Italy. Relatives persuaded Brumidi to go to America. He arrived in New York on September 18, 1852. He painted portraits for a living until friends informed him that artists were being hired in Washington, D. C.

In the President's Room Brumidi painted portraits of George Washington and his first cabinet. He was past sixty when he began painting huge figures across the concave interior of the Capitol dome. Lying upon his back upon a scaffold ten hours a day, Brumidi painted the figures in scale so they looked lifesize from the floor 180 feet below.

In 1877, when Brumidi was seventy-five years old he began painting in fresco fifteen scenes of historical events in the immense band that encircled the rotunda balcony.

Brumidi used the same technique as Michelangelo, a steel point to trace the outline of the figure in fresh plaster and quickly apply mineral colors. The colors are absorbed and do not reveal their full effect until the plaster is dry. The artist must be very good, for an error means he must start the entire section over again.

Brumidi failed to show up for work February 19, 1880. He hadn't missed a day of work since he was hired in 1855. He painted through the administrations of Presidents Pierce, Buchanan, Lincoln, Johnson, Grant, and Hayes—twenty-five years of labor!

A messenger was sent to Brumidi's apartment and found the artist had died during the night. Officials were amazed when it was learned that Brumidi died broke. An old ledger found beneath his bed revealed that Brumidi had donated all of his wages other than living expenses to orphans' homes and other charities to show his appreciation to the nation he loved so well.

In 1952, a delegation of Congressmen led by Speaker of the House, Sam Rayburn, visited the grave of Constantine Brumidi at Glenwood Cemetery in N. E. Washington. A bronze plaque was unveiled in honor of the Italian artist.

"Few people know that this artist devoted twenty-five years of his life making our Capitol beautiful," said Speaker Rayburn. "Today we pay long overdue tribute to an immigrant who had love and devotion for his adopted land. Constantine Brumidi was a dedicated and patriotic artist who left behind a great memorial, his beautiful paintings in the Capitol Building."

If Constantine Brumidi had been alive that warm spring day of 1952, he would have been speechless to have had such distinguished Americans paying him honor. But to Constantine Brumidi himself the greatest honor would have come in the moment when the Speaker planted an American flag to wave gently in the breeze above his grave.

Richard Barness

The Sublime And The Beautiful

I visited various parts of my own country; and had I been merely a lover of fine scenery, I should have felt little desire to seek elsewhere its gratification: for on no country have the charms of nature been more prodigally lavished. Her mighty lakes, like oceans of liquid silver; her mountains, with their bright aerial tints; her valleys, teeming with wild fertility; her tremendous cataracts, thundering in their solitudes; her boundless plains, waving with spontaneous verdure; her broad deep rivers, rolling in solemn silence to the ocean; her trackless forests, where vegetation puts forth all its magnificence; her skies, kindling with the magic of summer clouds and glorious sunshine;—no, never need an American look beyond his own country for the sublime and beautiful of natural scenery.

Washington Irving

Good Old Days

Things have changed greatly and still are changing, can they change much more? Can you think of any more improvements? My father liked his fireplace the same as I like my old iron stove, and now they have the gas and electric ranges, but I would not be surprised when the younger generation gets old, when people of coming generations, a hundred years from now, will look back upon us as primitives.

And yet I wonder sometimes whether we are progressing. In my childhood days life was different, in many ways, we were slower, still we had a good and happy life, I think, people enjoyed more in their way, at least they seemed to be happier, they don't take time to be happy nowadays.

Grandma Moses

Daniel Boone

Daniel Boone at twenty-one
Came with his tomahawk, knife, and gun
Home from the French and Indian War
To North Carolina and the Yadkin shore.
He married his maid with a golden band,
Builded his house and cleared his land;
But the deep woods claimed their son again
And he turned his face from the homes of men.
Over the Blue Ridge, dark and lone,
The Mountains of Iron, the Hills of Stone,
Braving the Shawnee's jealous wrath,
He made his way on the Warrior's Path.
Alone he trod the shadowed trails;
But he was lord of a thousand vales
As he roved Kentucky, far and near,
Hunting the buffalo, elk, and deer.
What joy to see, what joy to win
So fair a land for his kith and kin,
Of streams unstained and woods unhewn!
"Elbow room!" laughed Daniel Boone.

On the Wilderness Road that his axmen made
The settlers flocked to the first stockade;
The deerskin shirts and the coonskin caps
Filed through the glens and the mountain gaps;
And hearts were high in the fateful spring
When the land said" Nay!" to the stubborn king.
While the men of the East of farm and town
Strove with the troops of the British Crown,
Daniel Boone from a surge of hate
Guárded a nation's westward gate.
Down in the fort in a wave of flame
The Shawnee horde and the Mingo came,
And the stout logs shook in a storm of lead;
But Boone stood firm and the savage fled.
Peace! And the settlers flocked anew,
The farm lands spread, the town lands grew;
But Daniel Boone was ill at ease
When he saw the smoke in his forest trees.
"There'll be no game in the country soon.
Elbow room!" cried Daniel Boone.

Straight as a pine at sixty-five—
Time enough for a man to thrive—
He launched his bateau on Ohio's breast
And his heart was glad as he oared it west;
There were kindly folk and his own true blood
Where great Missouri rolls his flood;
New woods, new streams, and room to spare,
And Daniel Boone found comfort there.
Yet far he ranged toward the sunset still,
Where the Kansas runs and the Smoky Hill,
And the prairies toss, by the south wind blown:
And he killed his bear on the Yellowstone
But ever he dreamed of new domains
With vast woods and wider plains;
Ever he dreamed of a world-to-be
Where there are no bounds and the soul is free.
At fourscore-five, still stout and hale,
He heard a call to a farther trail;
So he turned his face where the stars are strewn;
"Elbow room!" sighed Daniel Boone.

Arthur Guiterman

Prayer Of A Beginning Teacher

Dear God, I humbly pray
　　That thou, with each passing day
　　Wilt give me courage, wisdom true,
To meet each problem, see it through—
　　With wisdom and justice to teach each child
　　To recognize the things worthwhile.
Help me to start them on the way
　　To clean, brave living—day by day,
　　So that tomorrow for each one
　　Will be met squarely—and be won—
And as I help each little child
　　To learn to love the things worthwhile,
　　Lord, help me to be true;
　　For I am just beginning, too.

Ouida Smith Dunnam

Principles Of Manhood

When a teacher of the future comes to point out to the youth of America how the highest rewards of intellect and devotion can be gained, he may say to them—not by subtlety and intrigue, not by wire-pulling and demagoguery, not by shiftiness in following expediency; but by being firm in devotion to the principles of manhood and the courage of righteousness in public life; by being a man without guile, without fear, without selfishness, and with devotion to duty, devotion to his country and his God.

Elihu Root

GOLDEN THOUGHTS

A boy has two jobs. One is just being a boy. The other is growing up to be a man.

Herbert Hoover

Be still and know the beauty of the forest,
Tall giants that have stood some thousand years
Make not a sound in all their massive splendor—
This peace is ours, and hushed are all our fears.

Eleanor Hillemann

The Old Oaken Bucket

How dear to this heart are the scenes of my childhood,
    When fond recollection presents them to view!—
The orchard, the meadow, the deep-tangled wildwood,
    And every loved spot which my infancy knew!
The wide-spreading pond, and the mill that stood by it;
    The bridge, and the rock where the cataract fell;
The cot of my father, the dairy-house nigh it;
    And e'en the rude bucket that hung in the well.
The old oaken bucket, the iron-bound bucket,
    The moss-covered bucket, which hung in the well.

That moss-covered vessel I hailed as a treasure;
    For often at noon, when returned from the field,
I found it the source of an exquisite pleasure—
    The purest and sweetest that Nature can yield.
How ardent I seized it, with hands that were glowing,
    And quick to the white-pebbled bottom it fell!
Then soon, with the emblem of truth overflowing,
    And dripping with coolness, it rose from the well—
The old oaken bucket, the iron-bound bucket.
    The moss-covered bucket arose from the well.

How sweet from the green, mossy brim to receive it,
    As, poised on the curb, it inclined to my lips!
Not a full, blushing goblet could tempt me to leave it,
    The brightest that beauty or revelry sips.
And now, far removed from the loved habitation,
    The tear of regret will intrusively swell,
As Fancy reverts to my father's plantation,
    And sighs for the bucket that hangs in the well—
The old oaken bucket, the iron-bound bucket,
    The moss-covered bucket that hangs in the well!

Samuel Woodworth

The Marine's Prayer

Almighty Father, let me be aware of Thy presence and obedient to Thy will. Keep me true to my best self, guarding me against dishonesty in purpose and deed, and helping me so to live that I can stand unashamed and unafraid before my fellow Marines, my loved ones and Thee. . . . If I am inclined to doubt, steady my faith: if I am tempted, make me strong to resist; if I should miss the mark, give me courage to try again. Amen.

Abraham Lincoln's Letter To Colonel Ellsworth's Parents

Washington, D.C., May 25, 1861

My Dear Sir and Madam:

In the untimely loss of your noble son, our affliction here is scarcely less than your own. So much of promised usefulness to one's country, and of bright hopes for one's self and friends, have rarely been so suddenly dashed as in his fall. In size, in years, and in youthful appearance a boy only, his power to command men was surpassingly great. This power, combined with a fine intellect, an indomitable energy, and a taste altogether military, constituted in him, as seemed to me, the best natural talent in that department I ever knew.

And yet he was singularly modest and deferential in social intercourse. My acquaintance with him began less than two years ago; yet through the latter half of the intervening period it was as intimate as the disparity of our ages and my engrossing engagements would permit. To me he appeared to have no indulgences or pastimes; and I never heard him utter a profane or intemperate word. What was conclusive of his good heart, he never forgot his parents. The honors he labored for so laudably, and for which in the sad end he so gallantly gave his life, he meant for them no less than for himself.

In the hope that it may be no intrusion upon the sacredness of your sorrow, I have ventured to address you this tribute to the memory of my young friend and your brave and early fallen child.

May God give you that consolation which is beyond all earthly power.

Abraham Lincoln

GOLDEN VERSE

The Blue And The Gray

By the flow of the inland river,
　　Whence the fleets of iron have fled,
Where the blades of the grave-grass quiver,
　　Asleep are the ranks of the dead:
Under the sod and the dew,
　　Waiting the judgment-day;
Under the one, the Blue,
　　Under the other, the Gray.

These in the robings of glory,
　　Those in the gloom of defeat,
All with the battle-blood gory,
　　In the dusk of eternity meet:
Under the sod and the dew,
　　Waiting the judgment-day;
Under the laurel, the Blue,
　　Under the willow, the Gray.

Sadly, but not with upbraiding,
　　The generous deed was done,
In the storm of the years that are fading
　　No braver battle was won:
Under the sod and the dew,
　　Waiting the judgment-day;
Under the blossoms, the Blue,
　　Under the garlands, the Gray.

No more shall the war cry sever,
　　Or the winding rivers be red;
They banish our anger forever
　　When they laurel the graves of our dead!
Under the sod and the dew,
　　Waiting the judgment-day;
Love and tears for the Blue,
　　Tears and love for the Gray.

Francis Miles Finch

Old Ironsides

Ay, tear her tattered ensign down!
Long has it waved on high,
And many an eye has danced to see
That banner in the sky;
Beneath it rung the battle shout,
And burst the cannon's roar;—
The meteor of the ocean air
Shall sweep the clouds no more!

Her deck, once red with heroes'
    blood.
Where knelt the vanquished foe,
When winds were hurrying o'er the flood,
And waves were white below,
No more shall feel the victor's tread,
Or know the conquered knee;—
The harpies of the shore shall pluck
The eagle of the sea!

O, better that her shattered hulk
Should sink beneath the wave;
Her thunders shook the mighty deep,
And there should be her grave;
Nail to the mast her holy flag,
Set every threadbare sail,
And give her to the gods of storms,
The lightning and the gale!

Oliver Wendell Holmes

Letter To Her Husband John Regarding Women's Rights

In the new code of laws which I suppose will be necessary for you to make I desire you would remember the ladies and be more generous and favorable to them than your ancestors.

Abigail Adams

Thanksgiving

One Day For Thanks

One day for giving thanks; and yet the sun
Sends abundant reassurance with each ray
Through all the year, and seed selects no one
Day's interval for growing want away
From earth; there is no stipulated hour
Alone of one brief season, when eyes may see
The intricate, slow opening of a flower
And the long rhythms of a wind-blown tree.
And since there are no set, specific times
When birds wake sudden music from still air
And children's lilting laughter soars and climbs,
How shall we set a time for thankful prayer?
How shall we pay, in one short interlude,
Our year-long debt of joyous gratitude?

Jane H. Merchant

Drink Deep, My Soul

Drink deep, my soul, of all the lavish glory
    That drowns my wond'ring gaze this autumn day;
What wild and swirling beauty spreads before me,
    Refreshment take—drink deep, drink deep, I say.

Through holy ground the winding pathway pushes—
    The handiwork of God is everywhere;
The hill and valley trees are burning bushes,
    Their flaming colors fill the crispy air.

The ling'ring bird still sounds its note of rapture,
    And sounds of music mingle with the sight;
Drink deep, my soul-this fleeting wonder capture—
    Too soon . . . too soon the long, dark winter night.

John W. Peterson

Quit Supposin'

Don't start your day by supposin'
   that trouble is just ahead.
It's better to stop supposin'
   and start with a prayer instead.
And make it a prayer of thanksgiving
   for the wonderful things God has wrought
Like the beautiful sunrise and sunset,
   "God's gifts" that are free
   and not bought—
For what is the use of supposin'
   the dire things that could happen to you
And worry about some misfortune
   that seldom if ever comes true—
But instead of just idle supposin'
   step forward to meet each new day
Secure in the knowledge God's near you
   to lead you each step of the way—
For supposin' the worst things will happen
   only helps to make them come true
And you darken the bright, happy moments
   that the dear Lord has given to you—
So if you desire to be happy,
   and get rid of the "misery of dread"
Just give up "supposin' the worst things"
   and look for "the best things" instead.

Helen Steiner Rice

Keep Gratitude

Keep gratitude alive in your heart. Try living on "Thanksgiving Street." Reckon up your mercies and you will feel an inner kindling of soul. People will be glad at the sight of you. And who knows? Perhaps even the heart of the Infinite Giver of every good and perfect gift will rejoice.

Aaron Meckel

The First Thanksgiving Proclamation (June 20, 1676)

On June 20, 1676 the governing council of Charlestown, Massachusetts, held a meeting to determine how best to express thanks for the good fortune that had seen their community securely established. By unanimous vote they instructed Edward Rawson, the clerk, to proclaim June 29 as a day of thanksgiving, our first.

The Holy God having by a long and Continual Series of his Afflictive dispensations in and by the present Warr with the Heathen Natives of this land, written and brought to pass bitter things against his own Covenant people in this wilderness, yet so that we evidently discern that in the midst of his judgement he hath remembered mercy, having remembered his Footstool in the day of his sore displeasure against us for our sins, with many singular Intimations of his Fatherly Compassion, and regard; reserving many of our Towns from Desolation Threatened, and attempted by the Enemy, and giving us especially of late with many of our Confederates many signal Advantages against them, without such Disadvantage to ourselves as formerly we have been sensible of, if it be the Lord's mercy that we are not consumed, it certainly bespeaks our positive Thankfulness, when our Enemies are in any measure disappointed or destroyed; and fearing the Lord should take notice under so many Intimations of his returning mercy, we should be found an Insensible people, as not standing before Him with Thanksgiving, as well as lading him with our Complaints in the time of pressing Afflictions:

The Council has thought meet to appoint and set apart the 29th day of this instant June, as a day of Solemn Thanksgiving and praise to God for such his Goodness and Favour, many Particulars of which mercy might be Instanced, but we doubt not those who are sensible of God's Afflictions, have been as diligent to espy him returning to us; and that the Lord may behold us as a People offering Praise and thereby glorifying Him; the Council doth commend it to the Respective Ministers, Elders and people of this Jurisdiction; Solemnly and seriously to keep the same Beseeching that being perswaded by the mercies of God we may all, even this whole people offer up our bodies and souls as a living and acceptable Service unto God by Jesus Christ.

John Winthrop

GOLDEN THOUGHTS

He who receives a benefit should never forget it;
he who bestows should never remember it.

Charron

Gratitude is the song of the soul in the presence of
the goodness of God.

W. T. Purkiser

A Memory Of The Heart

Dr. William L. Stidger relates that one evening during the depression of the 1930's, he was discussing the general situation with some friends. The outlook was gloomy. Banks were closed; thousands were out of work; and men by the scores, faced with the collapse of their paper fortunes, were taking their own lives.

"There isn't much to be thankful for," one of the company remarked.

Stidger said, "Well, I, for one, am grateful to Mrs. Wendt." He explained that Mrs. Wendt was a schoolteacher who thirty years before had gone out of her way to encourage him in his studies.

"Did you ever thank her?" someone queried.

Dr. Stidger admitted that he never had. But that very evening he sat down and wrote her.

In a few weeks a reply to his letter arrived, written in the shaky hand of an aged person. The letter read:

"My dear Willie: I want you to know what your note meant to me. I am an old lady in my eighties, living alone in a small room, cooking my own meals, lonely and seeming like the last leaf on the tree."

"You will be interested to know, Willie, that I taught school for fifty years and in all that time yours is the first letter of appreciation I have ever received. It came on a blue, cold morning and it cheered my lonely old heart as nothing has cheered me in many years."

W. T. Purkiser

Thanksgiving

They went to church that day in Plymouth town,
To thank God for His goodness. For they had
Known hunger, pain and want, gone thinly clad
Through iron winter, thrown the gauntlet down
To death himself, and let him take his toll,
And now they had won through. . . . And so they
  prayed
Their word of thanks, and stood up unafraid
And faced the future with undaunted soul.

Today we, too, look back upon a road
Blood-stained and dark, haunted by panic fears;
And we, too, thank our God because He showed,
Beyond the gloom and dusk of barren years,
Beyond the memories of pain and sorrow
The dawning of a glorious tomorrow!

Bruce Catton

Giving Thanks

I saw a bird at watering trough
Dip in his bill, and then fly off,
Trilling a song—his thanks, I think,
For that cold and sparkling drink.

I saw a child with an earnest face,
Sit with his head bowed, saying grace;
Voicing his childlike gratitude
For his simple and wholesome food.

I saw a woman, bent and old,
Thinly clad, and shaken with cold;
But she smiled as the sun set red—
"Thank thee for beauty, God," she said.

All through the year I have heard men pray,
Thanking thee, Lord, each worship day;
Lifting the old hymns, sweet and clear,
In town and city, far and near.

But on this one day set apart
For the thoughtful and glad of heart,
Lord, 'tis a beautiful thing to see
A grateful nation thanking Thee!

Grace Noll Crowell

The First Thanksgiving Proclamation Of The United States—1789

Whereas, it is the duty of all nations to acknowl-
edge the providence of Almighty God, to obey His
will, to be grateful for His benefits and humbly
to implore His protection and favor; and

*Whereas, both Houses of Congress have, by their
joint committee, requested me "to recommend to the
people of the United States a day of public thanksgiving and prayer, to be observed by acknowledging
with grateful hearts the many and signal favors of
Almighty God, especially by affording them an opportunity peaceably to establish a form of government
for their safety and happiness;"*

Now, therefore, I do recommend and assign Thursday,
the twenty-sixth day of November next to be devoted
by the people of these States to the service of
that great and glorious Being who is the beneficent
author of all the good that was, that is, or that
will be; that we may then all unite in rendering
unto Him our service and humble thanks for His kind
care and protection of the people of this country
previous to their becoming a nation; for the signal
and manifold mercies and the favorable interposi-
tions of His providence in the course and conclusion
of the late war; for the great degree of tranquility,
union and plenty which we have since enjoyed; for
the peaceable and rational manner in which we have
been enabled to establish constitutions of government for our safety and happiness, and particularly
the national one now lately instituted; for the
civil and religious liberty with which we are blessed, and the means we have of acquiring and diffusing
useful knowledge; and, in general, for all the great
and various favors which He has been pleased to
confer upon us.

*And also that we may then unite in most humbly
offering our prayers and supplications to the great
Lord and Ruler of Nations, and beseech Him to pardon
our national and other transgressions, to enable
us all, whether in public or private stations, to
perform our several and relative duties properly
and punctually; to render our National Government
a blessing to all the people by constantly being a
government of wise, just and constitutional laws,
discreetly and faithfully executed and obeyed; to*

*protect and guide all sovereigns and nations
(especially such as have shown kindness to us),
and to bless them with good governments, peace and
concord; to promote the knowledge and practice of
true religion and virtue, and the increase of
science among them and us; and, generally, to grant
unto all mankind such a degree of temporal prosper-
ity as He alone knows to be best.*

Given under my hand, at the city of New York, the
third day of October, A.D. 1789.

George Washington

GOLdEN VERSE

A Season Of The Heart

The frost-tipped leaves now lie in drifts
On lane and city street,
Their scarlet beauty tinged to bronze;
And earth and sky now meet
On far horizons dimmed to gray
Foretelling winter's cold;
A blue mist shimmers on the hills
Swept clean of autumn's gold.

The splendor of the harvest fills
The coffers of the land,
And grateful hearts give thanks for all
The bounty from God's hand.
The work of earth is finished now
And busy hands can rest;
Thanksgiving prayers are offered up
And every home is blessed.

But let us hold this thought before
November days depart . . .
Not just for now . . . Thanksgiving is
A season of the heart.

Catherine E. Berry

Beauty Is God's Handwriting

Oh, the splendor of the Universe! For many, Thanksgiving time is the most glorious of all the year. God has dipped his paint brush in His palette of colors, and splashed the hills and woods and fields with robes of saffron, and crimson, and gold, and yellow, and brown, and scarlet . . . The maples and chestnuts and oaks vie with one another in thanksgiving beauty. The sumac dazzles the eye with brilliance. The sunsets are too gorgeous for human description . . . In this amazing garden of beauty, our lips involuntarily sing forth praises of thanksgiving, like unto the psalmist:

> "Bless Jehovah, O my soul;
> And all that is within me,
> Bless His holy name."

Charles Kingsley

Praise, My Soul, The King

Praise, my soul, the King of heaven,
To His feet thy tribute bring;
Ransomed, healed, restored, forgiven,
Who, like me, His praise should sing?
Praise Him! praise Him! praise Him! praise Him!
Praise the Everlasting King!

Praise Him for His grace and favor
To our fathers in distress;
Praise Him, still the same forever,
Slow to chide, and swift to bless.
Praise Him! praise Him! praise Him! praise Him!
Glorious in His faithfulness!

Father-like, He tends and spares us;
Well our feeble frame He knows,
In His hands He gently bears us,
Rescues us from all our foes.
Praise Him! praise Him! praise Him! praise Him!
Widely as His mercy flows!

Henry Lyte

I Thank Thee

I Thank Thee, God, for these—the commonplace:
My home, my bed at night, a child's embrace;
A humble church where I may worship, too;
For rainy days, and little tasks to do.

I thank Thee, God, that such a lovely thing
As setting sun at end of day can bring
Me ecstasy; for loving friends who care;
I thank Thee for the privilege to share
Thy blessings; and assurance as I live—
I need but ask Thee, Lord, Thou wilt forgive!

Christine Grant Curless

Grant unto us with Thy gifts a heart to love Thee; and enable us to show our thankfulness for all Thy benefits by giving up ourselves to Thy service and delighting in all things to do Thy blessed will; through Jesus Christ our Lord. Amen.

The Book of Common Worship

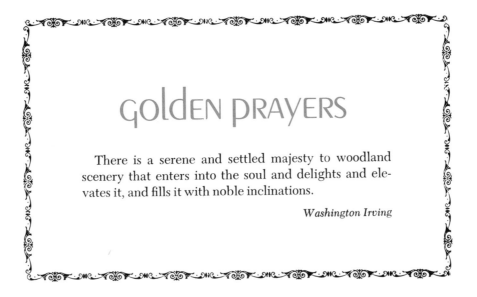

GOLDEN PRAYERS

There is a serene and settled majesty to woodland scenery that enters into the soul and delights and elevates it, and fills it with noble inclinations.

Washington Irving

Thank You Now

How long ago, it seems, we used to list
All of the gifts received we could remember
From those preceding months, late in November:
From valentines, and lilacs, April-kissed,
To emerald-and-golden days adored
And all the general blessings children name!
How long ago it was before we came
To our this-minute, whispered, "Thank You, Lord."

Perhaps we use it, knowing we'd forget
Much we had meant to thank You for—and yet
Whenever our gratitude at being blessed
With love and life and laughter and the rest
Wells up in us, and overflows, somehow
The words rise with it: "Thank You, thank You now!"

Elaine V. Emans

Thanks be unto God for His unspeakable gift.

II Corinthians 9:15

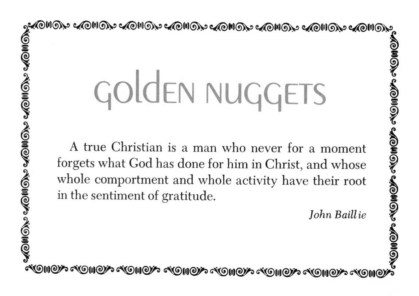

GOLDEN NUGGETS

A true Christian is a man who never for a moment forgets what God has done for him in Christ, and whose whole comportment and whole activity have their root in the sentiment of gratitude.

John Baillie

Keep Praying

It matters not how much we ask . . . When any prayer we speak . . . How many blessings for our friends . . . Or for ourselves we seek . . . God does not mind how often or . . . How pleadingly we call . . . Indeed He warmly welcomes our . . . Petitions, one and all . . . But we must understand that by . . . His wisdom great forever . . . Some prayers are answered very soon . . . Some later, and some never . . . For He knows what is best for us . . . And all for whom we pray . . . And whether He should help us more . . . Than we deserve today . . . And so each time we beg of God . . . Some favor to fulfill . . . Let us be patiently resigned . . . To His most holy will.

James J. Metcalfe

God is beside us each step
of the way
If only we lean on His arm
as we pray
His love is eternal and help
can be wrought
If faith is applied in each
prayer and each thought.

Author Unknown

I, do, therefore, invite my fellow citizens in every part of the United States . . . those at sea . . . those sojourning in foreign lands to observe . . . a day of thanksgiving and praise to our beneficent Father Who dwelleth in the heavens. . . .

Abraham Lincoln

My Thanks To Thee

I thank Thee for recurrent dawns,
For many stars, for many snows;
And for the shining unknown bird
That comes a single time, and goes.

Jane Merchant

The Touch Of God

I saw the frost upon the glass
    And marveled at the beauty there.
No artist's hand was seen to pass
    And paint for me the pattern fair.
The crystals gathered one by one,
    'Till frosted fairy tree and storm
Were fashioned as by magic done,
    With wondrous grace and lovely form.
The Myst'ry that perfumed the rose,
    The Life that thrust aside the clod,
The Skill this frosted pattern chose
    Bespeak to me the touch of God.

Clifton E. Rash

May God give us grateful hearts
And keep us mindful
Of the need of others.

Anonymous

An Ordinary Day

Today was just an ordinary day—
I went about my tasks the usual way;
The path was one that I had often trod,
But oh, the difference—
  Now I walk with God.

Today was just an ordinary day
And nothing special happened on the way,
But oh, the inner joy you didn't see,
Now that I know my Savior
  Walks with me!

Today was just an ordinary day,
The usual work, and then a bit of play,
But oh, the sense of peace at eventide
To know that God and I walk
  Side by side!

Helen Lowrie Marshall

A grateful thought toward heaven is of itself a prayer.

—*Gotthold Ephraim Lessing*

If a man measures life by what
  others do for him, he is apt to
be disappointed; but if he measures
life by what he does for others,
there is no time for despair.

William Jennings Bryan

To A Snowdrop

Lone flower, hemmed in with snows and white as they
But hardier far, once more I see thee bend
Thy forehead, as if fearful to offend,
Like an unbidden guest. Though day by day,
Storms, sallying from the mountaintops, waylay
The rising sun, and on the plains descend;
Yet art thou welcome, welcome as a friend
Whose zeal outruns his promise! Blue-eyed May
Shall soon behold this border thickly set
With bright jonquils, their odours lavishing
On the soft west wind and his frolic peers;
Nor will I then thy modest grace forget,
Chaste snowdrop, venturous harbinger of spring
And pensive monitor of fleeting years!

William Wordsworth

A Prayer For Patience

God, teach me to be patient—
Teach me to go slow—
Teach me how to "wait on You"
When my way I do not know . . .
Teach me sweet forbearance
When things do not go right
So I remain unruffled
when others grow uptight . . .
Teach me how to quiet
My racing, rising heart
So I may hear the answer
You are trying to impart . . .
Teach me to let go, dear God,
And pray undisturbed until
My heart is filled with inner peace
And I learn to know Your will!

Helen Steiner Rice

golden Thoughts

Gratitude is the heart's memory

Anonymous

The People's Thanksgiving

Not alone for mighty empire,
Stretching far o'er land and sea,
Not alone for bounteous harvests,
Lift we up our hearts to thee:
Standing in the living present,
Memory and hope between,
Lord, we would with deep thanksgiving
Praise thee more for things unseen.

Not for battle-ship and fortress,
Not for conquests of the sword,
But for conquests of the spirit
Give we thanks to thee, O Lord;
For the heritage of freedom,
For the home, the church, the school,
For the open door to manhood
In a land the people rule.

For the armies of the faithful,
Lives that passed and left no name;
For the glory that illumines
Patriot souls of deathless fame;
For the people's prophet-leaders,
Loyal to thy living word,—
For all heroes of the spirit,
Give we thanks to thee, O Lord.

William Pierson Merrill

The Pilgrim Fathers

O God, beneath thy guiding hand
   Our exiled fathers crossed the sea;
And when they trod the wintry strand,
   With prayer and psalm they worshipped thee.
Thou heard'st, well pleased, the song, the prayer:
   Thy blessing came; and still its power
Shall onward through all ages bear
   The memory of that holy hour.

Laws, freedom, truth, and faith in God
   Came with those exiles o'er the waves;
And where their pilgrim feet have trod,
   The God they trusted guards their graves.
And here thy name, O, God of love,
   Their children's children shall adore,
Till these eternal hills remove,
   And spring adorns the earth no more.

Leonard Bacon

Prayer

God of our fathers, give unto us, thy servants, a true appreciation of our heritage, of great men and great deeds in the past, but let us not be intimidated by feelings of our own inadequacy for this troubled hour.

Remind us that the God they worshiped, and by whose help they laid the foundations of our Nation, is still able to help us uphold what they bequeathed and to give it new meanings.

Remind us that we are not called to fill the places of those who have gone, but to fill our own places, to do the work thou hast laid before us, to do the right as thou hast given us to see the right, always to do the very best we can, and to leave the rest to thee.

Peter Marshall

Friendship

The World Would Be A Nicer Place
If We Traveled At A Slower Pace

Amid stresses and strains
　　much too many to mention,
And pressure-packed days
　　filled with turmoil and tension,
We seldom have time
　　to be "friendly or kind"
For we're harassed and hurried
　　and always behind—
And while we've more "gadgets"
　　and "buttons to press"
Making leisure hours greater
　　and laboring hours less,
And our standards of living
　　they claim have improved
And "repressed inhibitions"
　　have been freed and removed,
It seems all this progress
　　and growth are for naught,
For daily we see
　　a world more distraught—
So what does it matter
　　if man reaches his goal
"And gains the whole world
　　but loses his soul"—
For what have we won
　　if in gaining this end
We've been much too busy
　　to be kind to a friend,
And what is there left
　　to make the heart sing
When life is a cold
　　and mechanical thing
And we are but puppets
　　of controlled automation
Instead of "joint heirs"
　　to "God's gift of creation."

Helen Steiner Rice

True Happiness

Who would be happy every day,
Must give some happiness away.
If I give happiness to you,
I'm sure to find enough for two;
But if I please myself alone,
I find my happiness has flown.

The secret of a happy life,
Is not alone to keep from strife;
Nor to be simply cheerful, gay,
Though that is good in every way;
But if real happiness you'd see,
There must some self-denial be.

Howard W. Pope

Always There

Bless those folks who are "always there,"
    Steadfast, loyal and true,
Standing by and happy to share
    Your joys and your cares with you.

Those who stand on the side and cheer
    The runners in life's race,
Whose faith supplies the needed boost
    To keep that winning pace.

Bless those backstage people,
    Whose art no plaudits rouse,
But who provide the background
    For those who take the bows.

Bless them all—those quiet ones,
    Steady and staunch and square,
The little matches that light the stars—
    The folks who are "always there."

Helen Lowrie Marshall

Not In Anger

When Leonardo da Vinci was working on his painting "The Last Supper," he became angry with a certain man. Losing his temper he lashed the other fellow with bitter words and threats. Returning to his canvas he attempted to work on the face of Jesus, but was unable to do so. He was so upset he could not compose himself for the painstaking work. Finally he put down his tools and sought out the man and asked his forgiveness. The man accepted his apology and Leonardo was able to return to his workshop and finish painting the face of Jesus.

What Does Love Look Like?

It has hands to help others.
It has feet to hasten to the poor
and needy.
It has eyes to see misery and
want.
It has ears to hear the sighs and
sorrows of men.
That is what love looks like.

St. Augustine

GOLDEN VERSES

Not what we give, but what we share,—
For the gift without the giver is bare;
Who gives himself with his alms feeds three,—
Himself, his hungering neighbor, and Me.

James Russell Lowell

Blest

I breathe a prayer of gratitude for life,
For all that I have learned and comprehend,
And blest indeed am I if I have earned
The kind regard of an enduring friend.

Harold G. Hopper

Friendship

Oh, the comfort—the inexpressible comfort of
    feeling safe with a person,
Having neither to weigh thoughts,
Nor measure words—but pouring them
All right out—just as they are—
Chaff and grain together—
Certain that a faithful hand will
Take and sift them—
Keep what is worth keeping—
And with the breath of kindness
Blow the rest away.

Dinah Maria Mulock Craik

Tell God all that is in your heart, as one unloads one's heart to a dear friend. People who have no secrets from each other never want subjects of conversation; they do not weigh their words, because there is nothing to be kept back. Neither do they seek for something to say; they talk out of the abundance of their hearts, just what they think. Blessed are they who attain to such familiar, unreserved intercourse with God.

François de Fenélon

GOLDEN NUGGETS

A true friend unbosoms freely, advises justly, assists readily, adventures boldly, takes all patiently, defends courageously, and continues a friend unchangeably.

William Penn

The things that really help a person are those we do with him instead of for him. You cannot make a person's personality over; only the person himself, with God's help, can do that.

Derek de Cambra

I Would Be True

I would be true, for there are those who trust me;
    I would be pure, for there are those who care;
I would be strong, for there is much to suffer;
    I would be brave, for there is much to dare.
I would be friend of all—the foe, the friendless;
    I would be giving and forget the gift.
I would be humble, for I know my weakness;
    I would look up—and laugh—and love—and lift.

Howard Arnold Walter

The Glory of Life is to love,
Not to be loved,
To give, not to get,
To serve, not to be served;
To be a strong hand in the dark to another in the
    time of need,
To be a cup of strength to any soul in a crisis of
    weakness.
This is to know The Glory of Life.

Author Unknown

The Beloved Physician Of Labrador

He was three years out of medical school. His growing practice pointed to a future of fame, fortune and luxurious living. So far as material prospects were concerned, Sir Wilfred Grenfell in his youth looked toward a brilliant future.

But about this time he was challenged with an idea that completely revolutionized his thinking. Why not devote his medical skill to the people of Labrador where there was no doctor at all? If he did this, his own future would not be as comfortable as in Britain perhaps, but how could he put his own concerns above those of thousands of people who were suffering and dying for lack of the care and hope he could give them?

He learned that in order to bring healing and care to these deprived people —unfortunate people, most of whom could pay nothing for his treatment— he would often have to reach them over a frozen wilderness by dog sled with temperatures 50 degrees below zero.

Sir Wilfred accepted the challenge and landed in Labrador in 1892. He found a situation that would tax his staying powers to the limit. "Without doctors, nurses or hospitals," he said, "people just got sick and either lived or died according to whether their illness or their strength won." During the first short season he treated 900 patients, many of whom had never seen a doctor before.

The crop-growing season in Labrador was so short the people had very few vegetables. There was not a month of the year the temperature did not at times fall below freezing. For the most part, the people were fishermen. They lived on wild berries and wild game. Their diets were so unbalanced they suffered many diseases brought on by malnutrition.

Before taking his medical course in Britain, Sir Wilfred had at one time hoped to be a minister like his father, but had given up the idea. After arriving in Labrador he found that by giving the people there the benefit of his medical knowledge, he could witness for his Lord more effectively than by any other form of ministry.

During his 42 years of Labrador life, Sir Wilfred's deeds of mercy were accomplished under incredible hardships. He had to work with the crudest sort of facilities. On reaching one home at midnight he cared for a boy with a broken thigh. He laid the boy on a kitchen table to set the limb, thawing out a frozen board and planing it smooth to make splints.

Once while traveling by dog sled over the frozen wastes he lost his way. He spent several nights in the woods, and became so hungry he cut pieces of sealskin from his boots, boiled them over a fire and chewed them for whatever nourishment they could provide.

Another time, Sir Wilfred carried an axe to clear away brush and other obstacles ahead of the dogs. Once while crossing a frozen stretch of water he and the dogs broke through the ice. He hurriedly cut the dogs loose from the sled to keep them from drowning. He himself was thrown into the icy water but succeeded in reaching an ice pan where, clad in a sweater, he spent a day and a night before being rescued by a native.

114

The doctor's survival of the hardships under which he labored seemed miraculous. God took care of him for the job He wanted him to do. Sir Wilfred never failed to call on Him to see him through. "I have never seen real prayer go unanswered," he said, "and I have seen it remove mountains."

In some homes he and one or more native assistants did both the cooking and the nursing. On one trip he came to an isolated cottage where he found the mother lying dead on the floor and the father dying. Five little children sat and watched. Sir Wilfred and his native assistants buried the parents. Although too late to help father and mother, he was a godsend to the children. He cared for them until he could get a crude orphanage started.

Dr. Grenfell got very little in the way of money, but he treasured above everything else the love of the Labrador people. They would undergo grueling sacrifices for their beloved physician. Volunteers would sometimes go ahead of him and clear a path through a brushy countryside through which he had to travel with his dog team.

When Grenfell announced that he could no longer face the work he was carrying on unless he had a hospital, 100 men volunteered to help build one. They went with the doctor into the woods where they camped two weeks cutting trees for the building. The 36 by 36 foot building, though a crude arrangement, enabled the doctor to treat and cure many more of the sick. With the same kind of help he built other hospitals, orphanages and schools. He toured the United States and Canada raising money and enlisting other welfare-minded doctors and nurses in this labor of love. With money raised on speaking tours, he eventually built hospitals and orphanages equipped with the best facilities.

In some of his ministrations he rowed up and down the coast in an improvised hospital ship, giving people in need of medical aid a chance to come aboard. The ship was subjected to great danger along the stormy coast where many ships had been wrecked. But Grenfell faced the dangers calmly saying, "As the Lord wills whether for wreck or service I am about His business."

One time a woman climbed aboard with two blind infants. The mother said she had four other children and offered to give all of them to the doctor to save them from their miserable existence. The doctor added them to his orphanage collection. The two blind children were sent to a school in Halifax for the blind. An eye specialist whom Dr. Grenfell had brought to the country restored partial sight to both children. They became teachers at a little industrial center the doctor had helped develop along the coast.

Bringing an important improvement in the living standards of the people were short-season crops of vegetables and other food products that the doctor got started by bringing agricultural specialists to the country. The people began enjoying more healthful living with less disease. He started industries such as the making of pottery from native clay, toy manufacturing and rug making to provide employment and in this way too raised the standard of living.

Before Grenfell's death in 1940, he had multiplied the results of his work with the sick and disabled many times. He opened dental offices. One famous

Continued on Page 116

Continued from Page 115

eye specialist whom Grenfell induced to visit Labrador twice a year restored the sight of one man who had been blind 18 years.

The transition in Labrador that has taken place as a result of the work of Sir Wilfred Grenfell—and later the Grenfell mission—seems almost unbelievable. There were no medical or nursing facilities whatever when his work started. The 15,000 natives now have four hospitals, 17 nursing stations, and many orphanages. Many small industries are providing employment.

In a recent year a survey showed that 6500 patients were admitted to the hospitals and nursing stations for a total of 70,000 patient days. There were more than 900 obstetrical deliveries and 1100 surgical operations the same year. Sixty thousand visits were made to patient clinics and 15,000 to homes.

Although Sir Wilfred died in 1940, the International Grenfell Association that came into being as a result of his activities, operates many boarding and day schools. No longer are the sick and injured reached by dog sled which has to have the road cleared in front of it. No longer are individual settlements isolated for the greater part of the year. Not only can they be reached over good roads that were not in existence when Sir Wilfred's work started, but the Grenfell mission uses two aircraft. Planes are used as air ambulances to transport doctors, nurses, patients and supplies.

And as Dr. Grenfell looked back over his 42-year labor of love he felt he had been far more richly rewarded than by any material fortune he might have accumulated in Britain.

Ross L. Holman

It's Strange

It's strange that just a word of cheer
Can drive away a threatening fear,
A bright glow in a friendly eye
Can give us strength and make us try.

It's strange a walk in cool, crisp air
Can make our judgments clear and fair,
How whitecaps on a mighty sea
Can lift our soul and set it free.

It's strange that one who understands
Can take us to enchanted lands . . .
Where dreams come true, and each hard mile
We see, at last, was so worthwhile.

Hilda Mary Kerrigan

A Lovely Day

Actually, I couldn't say
What made this such a lovely day.
The air was chill, the clouds hung low,
Yet it was lovely—that I know.

Perhaps it was because someone
Smiled my way and brought the sun;
Maybe it was only that
A friend stopped for a little chat;
Or that a neighbor passing by
Called a warm and friendly "Hi!"

Possibly its special glow
Came from helping one I know—
Not much really—just a hand
To let him know I understand.

Nothing happened, actually,
To set this day apart for me.
Things went along the usual way—
But oh, it's been a lovely day!

Helen Lowrie Marshall

Patience is the quality which closed the gap between ourselves and others. It is a kind of heavenly courtesy which says, "I do not quite understand why you are as you are, but then I cannot understand myself; and since there is One who understands us both, let us extend to each other the patience He has had for each of us." Love without patience is not really love at all, but a shadowy vapor which will vanish at the first hot wind of reality, as the mists of night vanish when morning comes.

Eileen Gruder

Grant Me These Gifts

Grant me the gift of laughter, Lord,
　　And the countenance of a smile.
Let my heart be big and warm enough
　　To walk an extra mile
With a lonely friend who is worn and tired,
　　And perhaps has lost his way;
And I shall count these gifts worthwhile
　　At the closing of the day.

Grant me the understanding, Lord,
　　To keep my soul serene,
That I may share the strength of it
　　When shadows intervene
In the life of a friend whose courage lags,
　　As he walks the daily road,
For I would count it an honor, Lord,
　　To share another's load.

Velta Myrle Allen

golden thoughts

A friend may well be reckoned the masterpiece
of nature.

Ralph Waldo Emerson

What a superb thing it would be if we were all big
enough in mind to see no slights, accept no insults,
cherish no jealousies and admit into our heart no hatred!

Elbert Hubbard

A trusted friend is a sea of sincerity, a continent of
concern, a universe of understanding, and a galaxy of
generosity.

William Arthur Ward

To think without confusion, clearly;
To love your fellowmen sincerely;
To act from honest motives purely;
To trust in God and Christ securely.

Henry Van Dyke

The only rose without thorns is friendship.

Madeline DeScudery

Whatever of love has touched a man's life has been touched by God.

Eugenia Price

Shining Hour

Tell me again of days gone by,
Help me recall the sounds and songs,
What matter if we can't return,
Back to the place where the heart belongs!
Waste not your sighs on years grown old,
Weep not for faces of the past,
Speak not again of long lost dreams,
And sands of time that flow too fast!
Within the power of all men,
The vision of a shining hour,
In every memory there clings,
The sweetness of a faded flower!
And what the heart has loved the most,
CAN NEVER BE MISLAID OR LOST!

Grace E. Easley

One Of The Least Of These

I heard Him at the dawning
   Through the whispering of the breeze,
   In the singing of the robin,
   And the rustling of the leaves.

I found Him in the evening
   'Mid the fragrance circling wide,
   In the lily of the valley,
   And the honeysuckle vine.

I felt Him in the darkness
   When He touched my trembling hand,
   Led me through the valley shadows,
   Pointed to the Promised Land.

But I really never knew Him
   Till when filled with love and joy
   I had shared the words of Jesus
   With a hungry little boy.

Lucile H. Jones

The Whole Bit

Lord, help me to laugh and smile,
not because I have to
but because I love You.
Help me to love people,
not because it's my duty
but because You love them.
Help me to love them
   for what they are
   where they are.
Give me the confidence
to trust people and believe in them.
Give me the stamina
to share myself with them
     and to give all of myself to You.
Give me the nerve
to ask for Your directions,
    then make me a bonfire
    with Your love the flame.

Carol Spencer

Golden Prayers

English Air-Raid Shelter Prayer

Increase, O God, the spirit of neighborliness among us, that in peril we may uphold one another, in calamity serve one another, in suffering tend one another and in homelessness and loneliness in exile befriend one another. Grant us brave and enduring hearts that we may strengthen one another, till the disciplines and testing of these days be ended, and Thou dost give again peace in our time, through Jesus Christ, our Lord, Amen.

Anonymous

Lonesome

Dear Master, I am lonesome;
    Dear Master, speak to me!
I've been longing here at twilight
    For the voices o'er the sea,
And it seems as if my heartache
    Would be hushed, less piercing be,
If Thou, Lord, wouldst come still closer—
    I am lonesome; speak to me!

I've been thinking in the stillness,
    As I've watched the sunset glow
Die out yonder on the hilltop,
    Leaving naught but cold and woe—
I've been thinking of the faces
    That have come a-trooping by,
Old-time faces, long-time vanished,
    Leaving me to wait and sigh;

And I'm lonesome, Lord, I'm lonesome;
    Come Thou closer; speak to me,
For I'm listening here at twilight
    To the voices o'er the sea,
And it seems as if my heartache
    Would be hushed, less piercing be,
If Thou, Lord, wouldst come still closer—
    I am lonesome; speak to me!

Ralph Spaulding Cushman

The older I grow in years, the more the wonder and the joy increase when I see the power of these words of Jesus—"I have called you friends"—to move the human heart. To the rich and poor alike, to the learned and ignorant, they bring with them a message of peace and love. They are "spirit" and "life"; and the results that follow are manifest.

The awe that rises in our hearts when the knowledge dawns at last that he has said to us, "You are my friends," passes on into confidence and joy. That one word "friend" breaks down each barrier of reserve, and we have boldness in his presence. Our hearts go out in love to meet his love.

C. F. Andrews

Kindness

I have wept in the night
For the shortness of sight
That to somebody's need made me blind;
But I never have yet
Felt a tinge of regret
For being a little too kind.   *Anonymous*

❦❦❦❦❦❦❦❦❦❦❦❦❦❦❦

GOLDEN THOUGHTS

Keep well thy tongue and keep thy friends.

Geoffrey Chaucer

Hear no ill of a friend, nor speak any of an enemy.

Benjamin Franklin

Appreciation is love returned. It is man's best pay.

Lawrence Giles

❦❦❦❦❦❦❦❦❦❦❦❦❦❦

O God, who hast made of one blood all nations to dwell on the face of the earth, we beseech Thee to hear our intercession for all races and kindreds of men, that Thou wilt turn all hearts unto Thyself; and that, departing from everything that estranges and divides, we may by Thee be brought into unity of spirit, in the bond of peace; through Jesus Christ Thy Son our Lord. Amen.

The Book of Common Worship

The Key To Friendship

To enter friendship's door
I sought a key to fit;
I tried the key of wealth
But could not enter it.
I tried the key of fame,
And pleasure's golden key,
But friendship's door so wide
Would not unlock for me.
But when I tried one key
And gave the door a shove
I watched it open wide,
Because the key was love.

Perry Tanksley

Well, this is the end of a perfect day,
    Near the end of a journey, too;
But it leaves a thought that is big and strong,
    With a wish that is kind and true.
For mem'ry has painted this perfect day
    With colors that never fade,
And we find at the end of a perfect day,
    The soul of a friend we've made.

Carrie Jacobs Bond

Worship

I asked God for strength, that I might
    achieve.
I was made weak, that I might learn
    humbly to obey . . .
I asked for health, that I might do
    greater things.
I was given infirmity, that I might
    do better things . . .
I asked for riches, that I might be
    happy.
I was given poverty, that I might be
    wise . . .
I asked for power, that I might have
    the praise of men,
I was given weakness, that I might
    feel the need of God . . .
I asked for all things, that I might
    enjoy life,
I was given life, that I might enjoy all
    things . . .
I got nothing that I asked for, but
    everything I had hoped for.
Almost despite myself, my unspoken
    prayers were answered.
I am among all men, most richly
    blessed.

Author Unknown

Good Father, I believe that in Christ You
will heal all my weaknesses, and they are
many and great, many and great; but
Your medicine is even greater.

St. Augustine

A Hymn

Now we must praise the Ruler of Heaven,
The might of the Lord and His purpose of mind,
The work of the Glorious Father; for He,
God Eternal, established each wonder,
He, Holy Creator, first fashioned the heavens
As a roof for the children of earth.
And then our Guardian, the everlasting Lord,
Adorned this middle-earth for men.
Praise the almighty King of Heaven.

Caedmon

Faith is required of thee,
and a sincere life—
not loftiness of intellect,
nor deepness in the mysteries of God.

Thomas à Kempis

The form of God is unspeakable and indescribable, because the eyes of the flesh cannot see him. He dwells in glory incomprehensible, in magnificence unfathomable, in power incomparable. If I say he is Light, I speak of something he made; if I say he is the Word, I speak only of his origin; if I say he is Mind, I limit him to intelligence; if I say he is Spirit, I speak of his breathing; if I say he is Wisdom, I speak of his progeny; if I say he is Strength, I describe only his might; if I say he is Power, I speak only of his operating activity; if I say he is Providence, I limit myself to his goodness; if I speak of his Kingdom, I refer to his glory; if I call him Lord, it is because he is Judge; if I say he is Judge, it is because he is just and righteous; if I say he is Fire, I speak of his wrath; but if I call him Father, I have said it all.

Theophilus of Antioch

No Prayer Goes Unheard

Often we pause and wonder
  When we kneel down to pray
Can God really hear
  The prayers that we say . . .
But if we keep praying
  And talking to Him,
He'll brighten the soul
  That was clouded and dim,
And as we continue
  Our burden seems lighter,
Our sorrow is softened
  And our outlook is brighter
For though we feel helpless
  And alone when we start,
Our prayer is the key
  That opens the heart,
And as our heart opens
  The dear Lord comes in
And the prayer that we felt
  We could never begin
Is so easy to say
  For the Lord understands
And gives us new strength
  By the touch of His hands.

Helen Steiner Rice

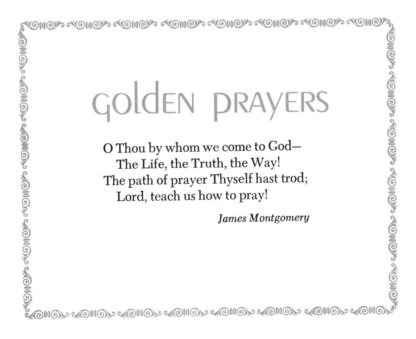

GOLDEN PRAYERS

O Thou by whom we come to God—
The Life, the Truth, the Way!
The path of prayer Thyself hast trod;
Lord, teach us how to pray!

James Montgomery

Father, To Thee

Father, to Thee we look in all our sorrow,
  Thou art the fountain whence our healing flows;
Dark though the night, joy cometh with the morrow;
  Safely they rest who in Thy love repose.

When fond hopes fail and skies are dark before us,
  When the vain cares that vex our life increase—
Comes with its calm the thought that Thou art o'er us,
  And we grow quiet, folded in Thy peace.

Naught shall affright us on thy goodness leaning,
  Low in the heart Faith singeth still her song;
Chastened by pain, we learn life's deepest meaning,
  And in our weakness Thou dost make us strong.

Patient, O heart, though heavy be thy sorrows!
  Be not cast down, disquieted in vain;
Yet shalt thou praise Him when these darkened furrows,
  Where now He plougheth, wave with golden grain.

Frederick L. Hosmer

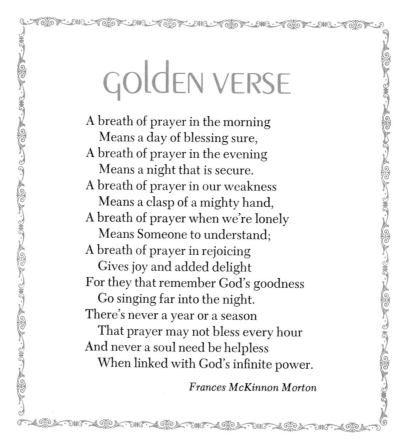

GOLDEN VERSE

A breath of prayer in the morning
  Means a day of blessing sure,
A breath of prayer in the evening
  Means a night that is secure.
A breath of prayer in our weakness
  Means a clasp of a mighty hand,
A breath of prayer when we're lonely
  Means Someone to understand;
A breath of prayer in rejoicing
  Gives joy and added delight
For they that remember God's goodness
  Go singing far into the night.
There's never a year or a season
  That prayer may not bless every hour
And never a soul need be helpless
  When linked with God's infinite power.

Frances McKinnon Morton

130

Trust In God And Do The Right

Courage, brother! do not stumble,
　　Though thy path is dark as night;
There's a star to guide the humble—
　　Trust in God and do the right.

Let the road be long and dreary,
　　And its ending out of sight;
Foot it bravely—strong or weary—
　　Trust in God and do the right.

Trust no forms of guilty passion—
　　Friends can look like angels bright;
Trust no custom, school, or fashion—
　　Trust in God and do the right.

Some will hate thee, some will love thee;
　　Some will flatter, some will slight;
Cease from man and look above thee—
　　Trust in God and do the right.

Firmest rule, and safest guiding,
　　Inward peace and inward light;
Star upon our path abiding—
　　Trust in God and do the right.

Norman Macleod

I prayed for faith and thought that some day faith would come down and strike me like lightning. But faith did not seem to come. One day I read in the tenth chapter of Romans, "Faith cometh by hearing, and hearing by the Word of God." I had [up to this time] closed my Bible and prayed for faith. I now opened my Bible and began to study, and faith has been growing ever since.

Dwight L. Moody

I remember one October night visiting a friend who was lying very sick. There was a full moon that night; and as I walked down the village street on my sad mission I felt the silvery beauty of it quiet my heart. The world lay lustrous. There was no scrawny bush nor ugly clod that was not transfigured in that glory. A little breeze over the brimming salt tide brought aromatic marshy odors. It seemed to me that some power was trying to make beauty take away my sadness. I found my friend not less aware than I was of the beauty of the night. He could look from his window and see the argent glamour of it all: how it flooded the gleaming tide with celestial lights; how it ran long white lances through the swarthy cedars; how it tinged with soft radiance the locusts and the mimosas. He felt the breeze too, and delighted in the odours that it brought of the happy world beyond his window. To my surprise, although he was very ill, he greeted me with a strangely elevated calmness and joy.

"I have been," he said, "in many waters, and they are still deep all about me. But God has been with me too. He has not failed me in my distress. Who but He could send this moonlight and this mocking bird singing. He brought them to me, and I think they bring Him near."

As I sat beside him, a mocking bird began to sing in the moonlight, chanting divinely. I know the song reached our spirits. On the table by the bed were all the necessities for a sick man; but he had small comfort from them. But the moonlight, and the hale fragrances, and the wild song of the bird— these brought peace to his heart.

Long aferward he said to me, "Do you remember that night? I thought it would be my last. But from the time the birdsong came through that window I felt that I would get well. I don't talk much about these things, but I felt that all that beauty and peace were really the love of God. I guess He does not love us with words: He loves us by giving us everything we need—in every way."

It must be as he said.

Archibald Rutledge

The Way

Sometimes I think I can't go on,
The hill's too steep, the road too long;
The valley's dark, I cannot see,
Grim, sabled night creeps over me;
The loneliness, the deep despair
Often are more than I can bear.
Then Christ comes in and takes my hand
And gently says "I understand.
Come, place your burden here on me,
I'll lead the way, I'll help you see."
And then I lift my heart in prayer
And find that Christ, indeed, is there!

Harriet McLuckie

They that go down to the sea in ships,
That do business in great waters;
These see the works of the Lord,
And His wonders in the deep.

Psalm 107:23, 24

You had no love to God, yet he has exercised unspeakable love to you. You refused to hear when God called, yet God heard you when you called. You have rejected Christ and set him at nought, and yet he has become your Savior. You have neglected your own salvation, but God has not neglected it.

You have set light by God, and have condemned him, but so great a value has God's Grace set on you and your happiness that you have been redeemed at the price of the blood of his own Son. You abused the infiniteness of God's mercy to encourage yourself in sin against him, yet God has manifested the infiniteness of that mercy in the exercises of it toward you.

You were ungrateful for past mercies, yet God has not only continued those mercies but has bestowed unspeakably greater mercies upon you. God has magnified his free Grace toward you because he has chosen you, and it has pleased him to set his love upon you.

You have reason, then, to open your mouth in God's praises, both here and to all eternity, for his rich and sovereign mercy to you.

Jonathan Edwards

golden thoughts

Ten minutes spent in Christ's society every day, ay, two minutes, if it be face to face, and heart to heart, will make the whole life different.

William Drummond

It is only when men begin to worship that they begin to grow.

Calvin Coolidge

Between the humble and the contrite heart and the majesty of heaven there are no barriers; the only password is prayer.

Hosea Ballou

The Love Of God

All things that are on earth shall wholly pass away,
Except the love of God, which shall live and last for aye.
The forms of men shall be as they had never been;
The blasted groves shall lose their fresh and tender green;
The birds of the thicket shall end their pleasant song,
And the nightingale shall cease to chant the evening long.
The kine of pasture shall feel the dart that kills,
And all the fair white flocks shall perish from the hills.
The goat and antlered stag, the wolf and the fox,
The wild boar of the wood, and the chamois of the rocks,
And the strong and fearless bear, in the trodden dust shall lie;
And the dolphins of the sea, and the mighty whale shall die.
And realms shall be dissolved, and empires be no more,
And they shall bow to death, who rules from shore to shore;
And the great globe itself, so Holy Writings tell,
With the rolling firmament, where starry armies dwell,
Shall melt with fervent heat,—they shall all pass away,
Except the love of God, which shall live and last for aye!

Bernard Rascas

This I Know

I know not by what methods rare,
But this I know—God answers prayer.
I know that He has given His Word,
Which tells me prayer is always heard,
And will be answered, soon or late,
And so I pray and calmly wait.

I know not if the blessing sought
Will come in just the way I thought,
But leave my prayers with Him alone,
Whose will is wiser than my own—
Assured that He will grant my quest,
Or send some answer far more blest.

Anonymous

All things are passing,
God never changes.

Henry Wadsworth Longfellow

When folks say that I walk alone,
With pity in their eyes,
I ever stand and stare at them
In wondering surprise,
Because they are too blind to see
That in each breathing clod,
In sun and rain in grass and trees,
I ever walk with God.

Edgar Daniel Kramer

A Prayer For The Young And Lovely

Dear God, I keep praying
For the things I desire,
You tell me I'm selfish
And "playing with fire"—
It is hard to believe
I am selfish and vain.
My desires seem so real
And my needs seem so sane,
And yet You are wiser
And Your vision is wide
And You look down on me
And You see deep inside,
You know it's so easy
To change and distort,
And things that are evil
Seem so harmless a sport—
Oh, teach me, dear God,
To not rush ahead
But to pray for Your guidance
And to trust You instead,
For You know what I need
And that I'm only a slave
To the things that I want
And desire and crave—
Oh, God, in your mercy
Look down on me now
And see in my heart
That I love you somehow,
Although in my rashness,
Impatience and greed
I pray for the things
That I want and don't need—
And instead of a crown
Please send me a cross
And teach me to know
That all gain is but loss,
And show me the way
To joy without end.
With You as my Father,
Redeemer and Friend—
And send me the things
That are hardest to bear,
And keep me forever
Safe in Thy care.

Helen Steiner Rice

Anna...The Creative Widow

Bracing herself with one arm against the marble column of Solomon's porch on the eastern side of the Temple in Jerusalem, the aging prophetess, Anna, turned to greet her elderly friend, Simeon, who was slowly climbing the steps from the street. Anna did not walk toward him, and Simeon did not hurry. Neither of them had ever hurried through the years of their lives. Too much of eternity had invaded their days for haste. They geared their comings and goings to the Lord God, depending, as children depend, upon His guidance —so abandoned to the divine will, so sensitive to the divine whisper that each lived hourly within the quiet order of holy rhythm.

Slowly, Simeon shuffled toward his devout friend, a smile crinkling the thin skin around his faded eyes. "Shalom, Anna," he said. "There will be a fine sunset for us to enjoy—just enough clouds to make the light glow."

"Yes, Simeon. Clouds are needed in order to make a sunset beautiful. Thanks be to the Lord our God for clouds, I say."

Simeon chuckled. "You've earned the right to say that, Anna. You've allowed the Lord God to make your life beautiful—and heaven knows it's been full of clouds."

She sighed. "There has been nothing about which to fuss, old man. I had seven years of happiness with my husband and all the other years between his death and my eighty-fourth birthday last week to enjoy the Lord God."

"You've been in the Temple most of the day, I suppose," Simeon said, pulling his cloak around his thin throat against the chill evening breeze.

"All day," she replied. "And all day my joy has grown. Oh, Simeon, old man—the Messiah comes soon! The Spirit of our God has assured me now, even as He has assured you, that I, too, will not die until I have seen Him." Her thin, veined hands were clasped and her face glowed.

"We are old enough, both of us, Anna, for the people to call us childish for our faith in the swift coming of the Messiah, but it is not we who are loose in the head—it is they. He comes, *very* soon now, He comes. I grow weaker daily. My time to leave draws closer. And as it does, so does the coming of our Messiah. God has promised I will not die until I have seen Him, and I am going soon."

Anna turned to look at her friend. "It is all joy, Simeon, going or staying because of the Lord our God."

Day after day, the old friends met somewhere in the Temple to speak of the coming of the promised Messiah. And on one certain day, as Anna prayed in the Court of the Women, the partitioned east portion of the inner court where both men and women could pray, she felt a gentle hand on her shoulder and turned to see her friend, Simeon, standing beside her.

"My old heart pounds this day, Anna," he whispered. "Could this be the day He will come? Do you have any word from the Lord God for me, my friend?"

Anna smiled. "Only the same assurance that it will be soon, Simeon."

"Then I will go to my own prayers and let you return to yours."

Anna watched him hobble away and tried to go back to her prayers, but her mind would not focus. A great excitement seemed to grip her so that her

Continued on Page 138

Continued from Page 137

bent old body shook. Suddenly she turned to look in the direction of the wide stair that led from the Court of the Women to the Court of the Gentiles, fully expecting to see a heavenly sign. All she saw was a simple Hebrew couple crossing the lower court, slowly, almost shyly, as though awed by the size and splendor of the Temple. In her arms, the young mother carried her baby. They have come for the purification, Anna thought, and was glad in her heart that one more man child would be the Lord's own. Anna had borne no children, and through the years, some of her happiest experiences had been to watch the young couples bring their sons to be dedicated to the Lord God.

She watched this humble, plainly dressed man and woman as they started up the stair to the Court of the Women, and then from the other side of the high partition she saw Simeon staring at the same two parents with their babe.

Anna watched Simeon cross the upper court and hurry dangerously close to the top of the stair as though he had expected this very man and woman at this very moment. He's going to fall! Anna caught her breath as Simeon lost his balance, then relaxed when the father of the child put his strong arm around Simeon to steady him. Unmindful of his narrow escape, Simeon raised both hands in the air and began to praise God in a loud voice, and Anna found herself hurrying toward the little group of people at the top of the stair —hurrying, with almost no pain in her stiff old legs.

When she reached them, the young mother was smiling as though for a deeper reason than that she held a new son in her arms, and Simeon was crying out: "Lord, now lettest thou thy servant depart in peace, according to thy word; for mine eyes have seen thy salvation which thou hast prepared in the presence of all peoples!"

Anna gasped as she saw her friend reach for the child, take him in his arms, and lift his radiant old face to God.

"For mine eyes have *seen* thy salvation . . . a light for revelation to the Gentiles, and for glory to thy people Israel!"

The young mother stood wide-eyed, marveling at what Simeon had said of her son.

"He knows, Mary!" her kind faced husband said. "This old man is a man of God; he knows the child is no ordinary child."

Anna stood transfixed, her eyes drinking in the beauty of the baby's face, as Simeon gently handed the child back to his mother, saying: "Behold, this child is set for the fall and rising of many in Israel, and for a sign that is spoken against—" And he stopped speaking and looked deeply into the young mother's eyes. ". . . and a sword will pierce through your own soul also, that thoughts out of many hearts may be revealed."

Anna saw the young woman frown slightly and look for some explanation from her husband. There was none. For a long moment, no one spoke, and then Anna, as though the very joy of heaven had been released within her, turned and hurried down the stair, across the Court of the Gentiles, and onto the porch, giving thanks to God and telling everyone she saw that the redemption of Israel had come to live among them!

Eugenia Price

My Act

Lord, when I kneel to pray
let it be a real thing,
not just a movement of the knee
triggered by habit
or imitation,
but an act that involves the heart,
the will,
in adoration.
Then when I rise, Lord,
let it be for real things.
Forbid my content
that a prescribed time for petition
has been fulfilled.
Make me restlessly alive,
aware
that my life has become an offering,
a prayer.

Jone Anderson

The Prayers I Make…

The prayers I make will then be sweet indeed,
If Thou the spirit give by which I pray:
My unassisted heart is barren clay,
Which of its native self can nothing feed:
Of good and pious works Thou art the seed,
Which quickens only where Thou say'st it may;
Unless Thou show to us Thine own true way,
No man can find it: Father! Thou must lead.
Do Thou, then, breathe those thoughts into my mind
By which such virtue may in me be bred
That in Thy holy footsteps I may tread;
That fetters of my tongue do Thou unbind,
That I may have the power to sing of Thee,
And sound Thy praises everlastingly.

Michelangelo

Fenestralia

Let me be
a stained glass window
in Your temple.
Take my dull
dark
ugly
blackened-purple panes
with no pattern
no meaning and
no life.

Let Your light shine through
translucent with color
line and truth.

Let me be a witness
of Your promise
that You will do
as much for any man
who will stand
in Your light.

Donna Hosford

Adoration

I love my God, but with no love of mine,
For I have none to give;
I love Thee, Lord, but all that love is Thine,
For by Thy life I live.
I am as nothing and rejoice to be
Emptied and lost and swallowed up in Thee.

Madame Guyon

The Bible is the greatest literary paradox the world has ever seen. It is the deepest and yet the clearest of books. Its greatest profundities have come from the simplest of men. It is most needed when it is least wanted. It dismisses with a sentence an entire nation to give us the message of a farmer. It ignores a king to tell us the story of a shepherd. It begins in a garden, it ends in a city. It begins with darkness, it ends in glory. It begins with a serpent, it ends with a Lamb. Early in its pages we find a creation ruined, late in its pages we see a new creation. In this book God is a consuming fire, and yet he says, "As one whom his mother comforteth, so will I comfort you."

You can get along without other books; this one you ignore at your peril. It is the book of warning. Do not add to it or take from it. It is older than nearly all the nations of today, yet it is fresher than tomorrow morning's dew. It is a rock for stability, a seed for growth, a sword for defense, and a spring for satisfaction. Its literature is ancient but prophetically modern. It tells the story of the past in terms of the future.

Will H. Houghton

He Knows

He knows it all—the winding path,
  The sky o'ercast and grey,
The steepness of the mountainside,
  The roughness of the way.

He knows it all—the haunting fear,
  The doubtings that distress,
The wond'rings and perplexities,
  And all the strain and stress.

He knows it all—each troubled thought,
  Each anxious wave of care,
And every burden, every grief,
  Or cross that thou dost bear.

He knows it all—thy weight of woe,
  Thine often tear-dimmed eye,
The stabbing pain, the slow, dull ache,
  And sorrow's broken cry.

He knows it all—but His to choose,
  And thine to take His choice!
He knows it all! He planned it so!
  Then trust Him, and rejoice!

E. Margaret Clarkson

What Is Prayer?

Prayer is so simple.
It is like quietly opening a door
And slipping silently into the very
. . . presence of God;
There in the stillness
To listen for His voice,
Perhaps to petition,
Or only to listen,
It matters not.
Just to be there
In His presence,
Is prayer!

Gertrude Wiebe

Truly my soul waiteth upon God.

Psalm 62:1

Singing
Praises in the night
To the great God
Of my salvation:
Miracle
Wrought in the light,
That he
Should stoop
To salvage a bit of clay
Like me.

Viola M. Berg

Christmas

The Shepherd Who Would Not Go

The Host of heaven and the angel of the Lord had filled the sky with radiance. Now they were gone, and the shepherds and the sheep stood under dim starlight. The men were shaken by the wonders they had seen and heard, and, like the animals, they huddled close.

"Let us go to Bethlehem," said the eldest of the shepherds, "and see this thing which the Lord hath made known to us."

The City of David lay beyond a far, high hill, upon the crest of which there danced a star. The men made haste to be away, but there was one called Amos who dug his crook into the turf and clung to it.

"Come," cried the eldest of the shepherds, but Amos shook his head. One called out, "It was an angel! You heard the tidings. A Saviour is born!"

"I heard," said Amos. "But I will abide."

The eldest walked back to him and said, "You do not understand. An angel commanded us. We go to worship the Saviour in Bethlehem. God has made His will manifest."

"It is not in my heart," replied Amos.

Now the eldest shepherd was angry. "With your own eyes," he cried out, "you have seen the host of heaven! And you heard, for it was like the thunder when 'Glory to God in the highest!' came ringing to us out of the night."

Another shepherd then broke in. "Because the hills still stand and the sky has not fallen, it is not enough for Amos. He must have something louder than the voice of God."

Amos held more tightly to his crook and answered, "I have need of a whisper."

They laughed and said, "What should this voice say in your ear? Tell us, what says the God of Amos, little shepherd of a hundred sheep?"

Meekness fell away from Amos, and he said in a loud voice, "To my hundred sheep, *I* am a saviour. See my flock. The fear of the bright angel and of the voices is still upon them. God is busy in Bethlehem; He has no time for a hundred sheep. I will abide."

This the others did not take so much amiss, for there was terror in all the flocks, and they knew the ways of sheep. Before the shepherds departed, each told Amos what he should do for the care of the several flocks. And yet one or two turned back a moment to taunt him, before they reached the dip in the road which led to the City of David. "We shall see new glories at the throne of God—and you, Amos, you will see sheep."

Amos paid no heed, for he thought, "One shepherd the less will not matter at the throne of God." Nor did he have time to be troubled that he was not to see the Child; there was much to be done. Amos walked among the sheep and made a clucking noise, which was a way he had, and to his hundred and

Continued on Page 146

Continued from Page 145

to the others it was a sound more fine and friendly than the voice of the bright angel. Presently the animals ceased to tremble, and they began to graze as the sun came up over the hill where the star had been.

"For sheep," said Amos to himself, "the angels shine too much. A shepherd is better."

With the morning the others came up the road from Bethlehem. They told Amos of the manger and of the wise men who had mingled there with shepherds. They described the gifts: gold, frankincense and myrrh. When they were done they said, "And did you see wonders here in the fields with the sheep?"

Amos told them, "Now my hundred are one hundred and one," and he showed them a lamb which had been born just before the dawn.

"Was there for this a great voice out of heaven?" asked the eldest of the shepherds.

Amos shook his head and smiled, and there was upon his face that which seemed to the shepherds a wonder, even in a night of wonders.

"To my heart," he said, "there came a whisper."

Heywood Broun

Song Of The Flax

They tell me I am only a form of grass,
But I am proud, remembering how it was
Centuries ago—did women not weave
Linen, as now? While Mary, quick to perceive

Its whiteness, wrapped Him in it,
  crowned with light.
And was it not her simple, pure delight
To wash it, keep it mended, and then dress
Her Babe anew in it? I must confess

This was long ago—my time of glory,
But I like to think I added to the story
Of Christmas, shielding from the
  stable's chill
The Child; that shepherds from a
  distant hill

And three kings, even, knelt, gave
  gifts, admired
The sleeping Lord, so lovingly attired!

Pauline Havard

O Christ, grant us thankful hearts today for thee, our choicest gift, our dearest guest. Let not our souls be busy inns that have no room for thee and thine, but quiet homes of prayer and praise where thou mayest find fit company, where the needful cares of life are wisely ordered and put away, and wide, sweet spaces kept for thee, where holy thoughts pass up and down, and fervent longings watch and wait thy coming. So, when thou comest again, O Holy One, mayest thou find all things ready, and thy family waiting for no new Master, but for one long loved and known.

Even so, come, Lord Jesus.

The Link

What Christmas Is

Christmas is love
tugging man back to God.

Molly Brooks

Let Us Be Quiet

Let us be still awhile this Christmas time;
O hurrying hearts restrain your restless beat;
Let us go journeying on some upward climb
Into the pure air, rarefied and sweet,
With the memory of another far-off night
When the Christ was born beneath a star's white light.

We have been loud and boisterous far too long—
Let us be silent, and perhaps we will
By listening hear the angels' heralding song
Ring clearly out above some distant hill,
And if we leave the clamoring word unsaid
A voice will guide us to Christ's manger bed.

It was a silent night, the night He came,
A holy night and may we keep it so;
There is one star God's own hand set aflame
Its lengthening rays will guide us as we go,
It is a silent fire, its rays point far
And through the centuries they will not dim
For every silver line of light directs
Mankind on the shining road that leads to Him.

Grace Noll Crowell

GOLDEN THOUGHTS

The sages and heroes of history are receding from us.
. . . But time has no power over the name and deeds and
words of Jesus Christ.

William Ellery Channing

I Would Give You This

Would that I could give each one of you a gift this Christmas season. I would wrap it with the glistening white of new fallen snow, and fasten it with a garland of evergreen. It would shine with the brilliance of the heavens lighted by the stars of December.

It would be a large package for it would contain many things. There would be a music box that would tinkle like the song of the tree sparrow intermingled with the sweet ones of the snowbirds. I would pluck some twigs of red maple, heavy with the red buds that cast a rosy glow over gray bark in winter sunlight.

Carols and hymns and dramatic music of great masters would be in your Christmas box. There would be a lullaby by the south wind in a forest of pines, and the lyrics of a woodland brook still pursuing its course between ice-encrusted banks. There would be a medley sung by the chickadee and nuthatch and titmouse, interrupted by the drumming of woodpeckers and the staccato chattering of squirrels. A crashing of cymbals and brass in a mighty symphony composed during a dramatic winter storm would stir your imagination.

Jack Frost would donate an etching wrought on glass, and the King of the North would fashion an alabaster work of sculpture as he moulded deep drifts of snow.

All day I would spend collecting these works of art for you. Last of all, I would tuck in some extra hours in your day so that you, too, could go outdoors to the storehouse where the work of our Maker manifests itself so abundantly. With the good earth beneath your feet and the broad expanse of sky stretching overhead, refreshment to body and mind would come to help you play your part in bringing peace on earth, goodwill among men.

Sunshine Magazine

All Hail, Thou Noble Guest

All hail, Thou noble Guest, this morn,
Whose love did not the sinner scorn;
In my distress Thou com'st to me;
What thanks shall I return to Thee?

Were earth a thousand times as fair,
Beset with gold and jewels rare,
She yet were far too poor to be,
A narrow cradle, Lord, for Thee.

Ah dearest Jesus, Holy Child,
Make Thee a bed, soft, undefiled,
Within my heart, that it may be
A quiet chamber kept for Thee.

Martin Luther

Christmas Parable

The stable boy had finished work that day,
Had filled the manger with new, fragrant hay,
Had fed the beasts, and usually would sleep
Snuggled for warmth among the placid sheep;
But not tonight, for he'd conceived a plan
To join a merchant's camel caravan
And travel to far places. He had heard
Exciting tales of cities, which had stirred
His longing for adventure. He would go
Where things were happening; his friends would know
Why he had gone. He often said to them,
"Oh, nothing happens here in Bethlehem."

He looked back once, before they traveled far,
And wondered vaguely: Why that brilliant star?

Velma West Sykes

Stopping By Woods On A Snowy Evening

Whose woods these are I think I know.
His house is in the village though;
He will not see me stopping here
To watch his woods fill up with snow.

My little horse must think it queer
To stop without a farmhouse near
Between the woods and frozen lake
The darkest evening of the year.

Robert Frost

I Know A Rose Tree Springing

I know a rose-tree springing
  Forth from an ancient root,
As men of old were singing.
  From Jesse came the shoot
  That bore a blossom bright
Amid the cold of winter,
  When half-spent was the night.
This rose-tree, blossom-laden,
  Whereof Isaiah spake,
Is Mary, spotless maiden,
  Who mothered, for our sake,
  The little child, new-born
By God's eternal counsel
  On that first Christmas morn.
O flower, whose fragrance tender
  With sweetness fills the air,
Dispel in glorious splendor
  The darkness everywhere;
  True man, yet very God,
From sin and death now save us,
  And share our every load.

Anonymous

TRuce In The FoRest

· When we heard the knock on our door that Christmas Eve in 1944, neither Mother nor I had the slightest inkling of the quiet miracle that lay in store for us.

I was 12 then, and we were living in a small cottage in the Hurtgen Forest, near the German-Belgian border. Father had stayed at the cottage on hunting weekends before the war; when Allied bombers partly destroyed our hometown of Aachen, he sent us to live there. He had been ordered into the civil-defense fire guard in the border town of Monschau, four miles away.

"You'll be safe in the woods," he had told me. "Take care of Mother. Now you're the man of the family."

But, nine days before Christmas, Field Marshal von Rundstedt had launched the last, desperate German offensive of the war, and now, as I went to the door, the Battle of the Bulge was raging all around us. We heard the incessant booming of field guns; planes soared continuously overhead; at night, searchlights stabbed through the darkness. Thousands of Allied and German soldiers were fighting and dying nearby.

When that first knock came, Mother quickly blew out the candles; then, as I went to answer it, she stepped ahead of me and pushed open the door. Outside, like phantoms against the snowclad trees, stood two steel-helmeted men. One of them spoke to Mother in a language we did not understand, pointing to a third man lying in the snow. She realized before I did that these were American soldiers. Enemies!

Mother stood silent, motionless, her hand on my shoulder. They were armed and could have forced their entrance, yet they stood there and asked with their eyes. And the wounded man seemed more dead than alive. "Kommt rein," Mother said finally. "Come in." The soldiers carried their comrade inside and stretched him out on my bed.

None of them understood German. Mother tried French, and one of the soldiers could converse in that language. As Mother went to look after the wounded man, she said to me, "The fingers of those two are numb. Take off their jackets and boots, and bring in a bucket of snow." Soon I was rubbing their blue feet with snow.

We learned that the stocky, dark haired fellow was Jim; his friend, tall and slender, was Robin. Harry, the wounded one, was now sleeping on my bed, his face as white as the snow outside. They'd lost their battalion and had wandered in the forest for three days, looking for the Americans, hiding from the Germans. They hadn't shaved, but still, without their heavy coats, they looked merely like big boys. And that was the way Mother began to treat them.

Now Mother said to me, "Go get Hermann. And bring six potatoes."

This was a serious departure from our pre-Christmas plans. Hermann was the plump rooster (named after portly Hermann Göring, Hitler's No. 2, for whom Mother had little affection) that we had been fattening for weeks in the hope that Father would be home for Christmas. But, some hours before, when it was obvious that Father would not make it, Mother had decided

Continued on Page 152

Continued from Page 151

that Hermann should live a few more days, in case Father could get home for New Year's. Now she had changed her mind again. Hermann would serve an immediate, pressing purpose.

While Jim and I helped with the cooking, Robin took care of Harry. He had a bullet through his upper leg, and had almost bled to death. Mother tore a bedsheet into long strips for bandages.

Soon, the tempting smell of roast chicken permeated our room. I was setting the table when once again there came a knock at the door. Expecting to find more lost Americans, I opened the door without hesitation. There stood four soldiers, wearing uniforms quite familiar to me after five years of war. They were Wehrmacht—Germans!

I was paralyzed with fear. Although still a child, I knew the harsh law: sheltering enemy soldiers constituted high treason. We could all be shot! Mother was frightened, too. Her face was white, but she stepped outside and said, quietly, *"Frohliche Weihnachten."* The soldiers wished her a Merry Christmas, too.

"We have lost our regiment and would like to wait for daylight," explained the corporal. "Can we rest here?"

"Of course," Mother replied, with a calmness born of panic. "You can also have a fine, warm meal and eat till the pot is empty."

The Germans smiled as they sniffed the aroma through the half-open door. "But," Mother added firmly, "we have three other guests, whom you may not consider friends." Now her voice was suddenly sterner than I'd ever heard it before. "This is Christmas Eve, and there will be no shooting here."

"Who's inside?" the corporal demanded. *"Amerikaner?"*

Mother looked at each frostchilled face. "Listen," she said slowly. "You could be my sons, and so could those in there. A boy with a gunshot wound, fighting for his life. His two friends—lost like you and just as hungry and exhausted as you are. This one night," she turned to the corporal and raised her voice a little, "this Christmas night, let us forget about killing."

The corporal stared at her. There were two or three endless seconds of silence. Then Mother put an end to indecision. "Enough talking!" she ordered and clapped her hands sharply. "Please put your weapons here on the woodpile—and hurry up before the others eat the dinner!"

Now, as Germans and Americans tensely rubbed elbows in the small room, Mother was really on her mettle. Never losing her smile, she went right on preparing dinner. But Hermann wasn't going to grow any bigger, and now there were four more mouths to feed. "Quick," she whispered to me, "get more potatoes and some oats. These boys are hungry, and a starving man is an angry one."

While foraging in the storage room, I heard Harry moan. When I returned, one of the Germans had put on his glasses to inspect the American's wound. "Do you belong to the medical corps?" Mother asked him. "No," he answered. "But I studied medicine at Heidelberg until a few months ago." Thanks to the cold, he told the Americans in what sounded like fairly good English, Harry's wound hadn't become infected. "He is suffering from a severe loss of blood," he explained to Mother. "What he needs is rest and nourishment."

Relaxation was now beginning to replace suspicion. Even to me, all the soldiers looked very young as we sat there together. Heinz and Willi, both from Cologne, were 16. The German corporal, at 23, was the oldest of them all. From his food bag Heinz managed to find a loaf of rye bread. Mother cut that in small pieces to be served with the dinner.

Then Mother said grace. I noticed that there were tears in her eyes as she said the old, familiar words, "*Komm, Herr* Jesus. Be our guest." And as I looked around the table, I saw tears, too, in the eyes of the battle-weary soldiers, boys again, some from America, some from Germany, all far from home.

Our private armistice continued next morning. Harry woke in the early hours, and swallowed some broth that Mother fed him. With the dawn, it was apparent that he was becoming stronger. Mother now made him an invigorating drink from our one egg. Everyone else had oatmeal. Afterward, two poles and Mother's best tablecloth were fashioned into a stretcher for Harry.

The corporal then advised the Americans how to find their way back to their lines. Looking over Jim's map, the corporal pointed out a stream. "Continue along this creek," he said, "and you will find the 1st Army rebuilding its forces on its upper course." The medical student relayed the information in English.

"Why don't we head for Monschau?" Jim had the student ask. "*Nein!*" the corporal exclaimed. "We've retaken Monschau."

Now Mother gave them all back their weapons. "Be careful, boys," she said. "I want you to get home someday where you belong. God bless you all!" The German and American soldiers shook hands, and we watched them disappear in opposite directions.

When I returned inside, Mother had brought out the old family Bible. I glanced over her shoulder. The book was open to the Christmas story, the Birth in the Manger and how the Wise Men came from afar bearing their gifts. Her finger was tracing the last line from Matthew 2:12: ". . . they departed into their own country another way."

Fritz Vincken

✦✦✦✦✦✦✦✦✦✦✦✦

Blessed Are The Meek

The miracle of Christmas is upon us again. . . . Yes, swaddling clothes, the manger, a little child—the world was indeed touched with humility. Among the dumb beasts God came to earth. As the world turns now toward the worship of power, we must remember that the first worshipers of the Christ-child were not the great and mighty, not the rich and noble. The oxen and sheep were his company, and the shepherds were his congregation. No power, no sword, no bombs, no guns, no books, no money . . . The mysterious lowliness of God.

F. L. Jensen

Midwinter

The speckled sky is dim with snow,
The light flakes falter and fall slow;
Athwart the hill-top, rapt and pale,
Silently drops a silvery veil;
And all the valley is shut in
By flickering curtains gray and thin.

But cheerily the chickadee
Singeth to me on fence and tree;
The snow sails round him as he sings,
White as the down of angels' wings.

I watch the slow flakes as they fall
On bank and brier and broken wall;
Over the orchard, waste and brown,
All noiselessly they settle down,
Tipping the apple-boughs, and each
Light quivering twig of plum and peach.

On turf and curb and bower-roof
The snow-storm spreads its ivory woof;
It paves with pearl the garden-walk;
And lovingly round tattered stalk
And shivering stem its magic weaves
A mantle fair as lily-leaves.

The hooded beehive, small and low,
Stands like a maiden in the snow;
And the old door-slab is half-hid
Under an alabaster lid.

All day it snows: the sheeted post
Gleams in the dimness like a ghost;
All day the blasted oak has stood
A muffled wizard of the wood;

Garland and airy cap adorn
The sumach and the wayside thorn,
And clustering spangles lodge and shine
In the dark tresses of the pine.

The ragged bramble, dwarfed and old,
Shrinks like a beggar in the cold;
In surplice white the cedar stands,
And blesses him with priestly hands.

Still cheerily the chickadee
Singeth to me on fence and tree:
But in my inmost ear is heard
The music of a holier bird;
And heavenly thoughts as soft and white
As snow-flakes, on my soul alight,
Clothing with love my lonely heart,
Healing with peace each bruisëd part,
Till all my being seems to be
Transfigured by their purity.

John Townsend Trowbridge

✦✦✦✦✦✦✦✦✦✦✦✦

Candlelight And Starlight

By candlelight and starlight came He then,
To kindle Hope of Peace in hearts of men.
And every Christmas candle on the sill
Reminds the world that Hope is burning still.
We see a promise in its glowing beam
Of one day the fulfillment of that dream.
By candlelight and starlight came He then;
May star and candle light His way again.

Helen L. Marshall

✦✦✦✦✦✦✦✦✦✦✦✦

The Lord of Christmastide entered into our life by lowly doors. And still He seeks the lowly doors: the door of the workshop, the door of the chamber, and all the unobtrusive doors of human friendship and regard.

John Henry Jowett

The Christmas Star

Stars rise and set, that star shines on:
Songs fail, but still that music beats
Through all the ages come and gone,
In lane and field and city streets.
And we who catch the Christmas gleam,
Watching with children on the hill,
We know, we know it is no dream—
He stands among us still!

Nancy Byrd Turner

Dedication

Holy Jesus, Thou art born
For my sake on Christmas morn.
Lord, as Thou art born for me,
I am born again to Thee.

Through the city and abroad,
Thou dost lead me unto God,
Wheresoe'er Thou leadest me,
Master, I will follow Thee.

To Thy love my love I give,
Thou dost die that I may live.
As Thou giv'st Thy life for me,
Lord, I give my life to Thee.

From the tomb I see Thee rise,
When the morning fills the skies.
Lord, as Thou art risen for me,
I will rise from death to Thee.

Victoria Saffelle Johnson

Sleep, My Babe

Hush, my dear, lie still and slumber,
  Holy angels guard thy bed!
Heavenly blessings without number
  Gently falling on thy head.

Sleep, my babe; thy food and raiment,
  House and home, thy friends provide;
All without thy care and payment,
  All thy wants are well supplied.

How much better thou'rt attended
  Than the Son of God could be
When from heaven he descended
  And became a child like thee.

Soft and easy is thy cradle;
  Coarse and hard thy Saviour lay,
When his birthplace was a stable
  And his softest bed was hay.

See the lovely Babe adressing;
  Lovely Infant, how he smiled!
When he wept, the mother's blessing
  Soothed and hushed the holy Child.

Lo, he slumbers in his manger,
  Where the hornèd oxen fed;
—Peace, my darling! here's no danger;
  Here's no ox a-near thy bed.

Mayst thou live to know and fear him,
  Trust and love him all thy days:
Then go dwell for ever near him,
  See his face and sing his praise.

Isaac Watts

From Little Women—A Merry Christmas

Jo was the first to wake in the gray dawn of Christmas morning. No stockings hung at the fireplace, and for a moment she felt as much disappointed as she did long ago, when her little sock fell down because it was so crammed with goodies. Then she remembered her mother's promise and, slipping her hand under her pillow, drew out a little crimson-covered book. She knew it very well, for it was that beautiful old story of the best life ever lived, and Jo felt that it was a true guidebook for any pilgrim going the long journey. She woke Meg with a "Merry Christmas," and bade her see what was under her pillow. A green-covered book appeared, with the same picture inside, and a few words written by her mother, which made their one present very precious in their eyes. Presently Beth and Amy woke to rummage and find their little books also—one dove-colored, the other blue—and all sat looking at and talking about them, while the east grew rosy with the coming day.

In spite of her small vanities, Margaret had a sweet and pious nature, which unconsciously influenced her sisters, especially Jo, who loved her very tenderly, and obeyed her because her advice was so gently given.

"Girls," said Meg seriously, looking from the tumbled head beside her to the two little nightcapped ones in the room beyond, "Mother wants us to read and love and mind these books, and we must begin at once. We used to be faithful about it, but since Father went away and all this war troubled us, we have neglected many things. You can do as you please, but I shall keep my book on the table here and read a little every morning as soon as I wake, for I know it will do me good and help me through the day."

Then she opened her new book and began to read. Jo put her arm around her and, leaning cheek to cheek, read also, with the quiet expression so seldom seen on her restless face.

"How good Meg is! Come, Amy, let's do as they do. I'll help you with the hard words, and they'll explain things if we don't understand," whispered Beth, very much impressed by the pretty books and her sisters' example.

"I'm glad mine is blue," said Amy. And then the rooms were very still while the pages were softly turned, and the winter sunshine crept in to touch the bright heads and serious faces with a Christmas greeting.

"Where is mother?" asked Meg, as she and Jo ran down to thank her for their gifts, half an hour later.

"Goodness only knows. Some poor creeter come a-beggin', and your ma went straight off to see what was needed. There never was such a woman for givin' away vittles and drink, clothes and firin'," replied Hannah, who had lived with the family since Meg was born, and was considered by them all more as a friend than a servant.

"She will be back soon, I think, so fry your cakes, and have everything ready," said Meg, looking over the presents which were collected in a basket and kept under the sofa, ready to be produced at the proper time. "Why, where is Amy's bottle of cologne?" she added, as the little flask did not appear.

"She took it out a minute ago, and went off with it to put a ribbon on it, or some such notion," replied Jo, dancing about the room to take the first stiffness off the new army slippers.

"How nice my handkerchiefs look, don't they? Hannah washed and ironed them for me, and I marked them all myself," said Beth, looking proudly at the somewhat uneven letters which had cost her such labor.

"Bless the child! She's gone and put 'Mother' on them instead of 'M. March.' How funny!" cried Jo, taking up one.

"Isn't it right? I thought it was better to do it so, because Meg's initials are M. M., and I don't want anyone to use these but Marmee," said Beth, looking troubled.

"It's all right, dear, and a very pretty idea—quite sensible, too, for no one can ever mistake now. It will please her very much, I know," said Meg, with a frown for Jo and a smile for Beth.

"There's Mother. Hide the basket, quick!" cried Jo, as a door slammed and steps sounded in the hall.

Amy came in hastily, and looked rather abashed when she saw her sisters all waiting for her.

"Where have you been, and what are you hiding behind you?" asked Meg, surprised to see, by her hood and cloak, that lazy Amy had been out so early.

"Don't laugh at me, Jo! I didn't mean anyone should know till the time came. I only meant to change the little bottle for a big one, and I gave all my money to get it, and I'm truly trying not to be selfish any more."

As she spoke, Amy showed the handsome flask which replaced the cheap one, and looked so earnest and humble in her little effort to forget herself that Meg hugged her on the spot, and Jo pronounced her "a trump," while Beth ran to the window, and picked her finest rose to ornament the stately bottle.

"You see I felt ashamed of my present, after reading and talking about being good this morning, so I ran round the corner and changed it the minute I was up: and I'm so glad, for mine is the handsomest now."

Another bang of the street door sent the basket under the sofa, and the girls to the table, eager for breakfast.

"Merry Christmas, Marmee! Many of them! Thank you for our books; we read some, and mean to everyday," they cried, in chorus.

"Merry Christmas, little daughters! I'm glad you began at once, and hope you will keep on. But I want to say one word before we sit down. Not far away from here lies a poor woman with a little newborn baby. Six children are huddled into one bed to keep from freezing, for they have no fire. There is nothing to eat over there, and the oldest boy came to tell me they were suffering hunger and cold. My girls, will you give them your breakfast as a Christmas present?"

They were all unusually hungry, having waited nearly an hour, and for a minute no one spoke—only a minute, for Jo exclaimed impetuously, "I'm so glad you came before we began!"

"May I go and help carry the things to the poor little children?" asked Beth eagerly.

"I shall take the cream and the muffins," added Amy, heroically giving up the articles she most liked.

Meg was already covering the buckwheats, and piling the bread into one big plate.

Continued on Page 160

Heaven

Song of the Creatures

Most high, almighty, good Lord,
    to You belongs praise, glory, honor, all blessings—
    to You alone, most high, belongs all reverence.
    No man can fully speak of all Your wonders.

Be praised, my Lord, with all Your creation—
    especially our brother the sun,
    who brings us day and light:
    He is beautiful and radiant with splendor.
    Most High, he is a symbol of You!

Be praised, my Lord, for our sister the moon and the stars:
    You have placed them in the heavens—clear, priceless, and
        beautiful.
Be praised, my Lord, for our brother the wind and for air,
    good weather, and seasons through which your whole
    creation lives.

Be praised, my Lord for our sister water,
    so useful, humble, precious, and chaste.
Be praised, my Lord for our brother fire,
    who brightens the darkness of night.
    He is beautiful, happy, robust and strong.
Be praised, my Lord, for our sister mother earth:
    she supports, nourishes, and gives forth vegetations—
    colorful flowers and grass.
Be praised, my Lord, for all those who forgive and understand
    one another for love of You—
    Those who bear sickness and suffering.
Happy are those who live at peace with one another.
They shall receive a crown from the Most High.

Be praised, my Lord, for our sister bodily Death,
    from whom no man can escape.
      How sad those who die without you!
      Happy are those who follow Your holy will—
        the second death shall be powerless to harm them.

Praise, blessings, thanksgiving to my Lord—
Let us serve Him with great love.

St. Francis

My soul is full of whispered song,
My blindness is my sight;
The shadows that I feared so long
Are all alive with light.

Alice Cary

Jesus said that He was the truth, and that the truth would make us free. Free from what? All over the world young people are shouting, "Freedom! Freedom! Freedom!" If we are in Christ, no matter who we are or what our national origin, we are free. Our spirit is free: free from the penalty of sin; we will never have to go to hell. We will never have to face the judgment of God if we are in Christ. We are also free from the power of sin. Sin will no longer have the mastery over us. And one day we will be free from the very presence of sin, for when we die and go to heaven there will be no sin there.

Billy Graham

The Passionate Man's Pilgrimage

Give me my scallop-shell of quiet,
My staff of faith to walk upon,
My scrip of joy, immortal diet,
My bottle of salvation,
My gown of glory, hope's true gage,
And thus I'll take my pilgrimage.

Sir Walter Raleigh

Golden Thoughts

Glorious indeed is the world of God around us, but more glorious the will of God within us.

Henry Wadsworth Longfellow

The Bible is a window in this prison-world, through which we may look into eternity.

Timothy Dwight

To gaze upon a beautiful sunset is to look through the gates of heaven.

Sir John Lubbock

One day I was sitting at my desk when our four-year-old walked through the room trying to thread a needle. If you have never witnessed a small child threading a needle, or attempting to do so, you are in for one of life's great frustrating experiences. The end of the thread was blunt and frazzled, and the needle in her other hand was turned sideways and unsteady in her grasp. My inclination was to snatch it away from her and do it myself. Watching her miss the target over and over again was like listening to a musical number with a dissonant ending; you want to rush to the piano and play the last chord so your soul might rest in peace.

As I watched her, I started to think about the number of times God must want to interrupt what I'm doing and do it Himself. But He is patient. I decided to let her keep trying. Finally, she said, "Daddy, would you do it for me?" I exhaled with satisfaction and relief, took the needle and thread, wet and twisted the thread, inserted it through the needle's eye, and returned it to her. She thanked me and proceeded to play.

Sometimes the Lord lets us get to the end of our rope on a project or ambition because He loves us too much to interfere. If He were to intervene, we would never learn. But once I have tried and failed, and then give it to Him, I know the next time to trust Him with it from the start. God's love is patient, and His patience with me allows me to discover for myself that I can trust Him completely.

Peter Gilquist

A Season Of Life And Death

There is no shadowed valley, no whimper, as the earth's northern half leans toward death this fall. The retreating sun offers neither repentance for the scorching heat just past nor apology for the cold to come. Rather it goes haughtily, flashing gold and russet leaves at the birds in battle formation and the brisk wind's icy darts chasing it south of the equator. It goes majestically, touching its lustrous scepter to autumn's abundance, grandly declaring that bare limbs and brown meadows are not tombstones to decay but seeds of new life.

"The hour that gives us life begins to take it away," Seneca wrote, and only the advance of God's Son can reverse the trend. "He who hears my word and believes him who sent me," Jesus said, "has passed from death to life."

Christianity Today

Golden Verse

On A Lonely Hill

On a lonely hill I stood alone
   Against a mourning sky,
In a grief-filled world I'd never known
   With none to hear my cry.

Racked with pain, heart-broken, ill,
   I stood alone with my loss,
Till it seemed I saw another hill
   And a Man on a cruel cross.

He, too, had stood on a lonely hill
   In pain that would not cease,
And I heard Him say, "My child, be still,
   I give to you My peace."

"Not as the world gives, do I give—
   The world may not understand—
But I say unto you that you can live
   With this grief—if you take My hand."

I came down out of the lonely hill,
   And my sorrow found release—
My hand in His, my will His Will,
   And in my heart His peace.

Helen Lowrie Marshall

To Comfort All That Mourn

Most people accept intellectually a belief in some kind of life after death. But usually it remains a theoretical belief until death invades one's immediate family circle.

Then at the time of the funeral, we are handed the victory. The working through of the specific problems that sorrow brings must come later.

Many know that initial victory. As with all God's gifts, we do nothing to earn or to deserve it. Undoubtedly a loving Father knows that without this kind of help, many of us could never withstand the emotional shock, would never even be able to get through the funeral.

At that time, the first need of the bereaved person is for comfort—just plain comfort. In sorrow, we are all like little children, hurt children who yearn to creep into a mother's arms and rest there; have her stroke our foreheads and speak softly to us as she used to do. But, of course, that is impossible; we are grown men and women. Yet the need for comfort remains.

Our God has promised precisely that . . . "Comfort ye, comfort ye my people, saith your God . . ." "For thus saith the Lord . . . As one whom his mother comforteth, so will I comfort you. . . ."

Strangely in my case I was given the beginning of that experience of comfort a few hours prior to my husband's death. That morning Peter had wakened about three-thirty with severe pains in his arms and chest. The doctor had come as quickly as he could. He had insisted that Dr. Marshall be taken immediately to the hospital.

As we had waited for the ambulance, Peter had looked up at me through his pain and said, "Catherine, don't try to come with me. We mustn't leave Wee Peter alone in this big house. You can come to the hospital in the morning."

Reluctantly I had agreed. I knew that he was right, though I wanted so much to be with him.

After the ambulance had come and gone, I went back upstairs and sank to my knees beside the bed. There was the need for prayer, for this was an emergency indeed. It could mean only one thing—another massive heart attack. But how was I to pray? Swirling emotions had plunged my mind into utter confusion.

Suddenly the unexpected happened. Over the turbulent emotions there crept a strange all-pervading peace. And through and around me flowed love as I had never before experienced it. It was as if body and spirit were floating on a cloud, resting—as if Someone who loved me very much were wrapping me round and round with His love.

Continued on Page 168

Continued from Page 167

I knelt there marveling at what was happening. I had done nothing, said nothing, to bring it about. Through my mind trooped a quick procession of thoughts . . . the Three Persons of the Godhead . . . Father, Son and Holy Spirit. . . . Sometimes I've known the spirit within as a nudge, as direction, or reminder, or conscience. . . . Once that was the turning point in my long illness. . . . But this is different . . . this must be the Father. . . . Maybe this is what the Bible means by that lovely statement—"underneath are the everlasting arms." That describes exactly what I'm feeling. . . .

But what did this mean in relation to Peter, his ailing heart, and the emergency that threatened us? I thought it meant that everything was going to be all right, that Peter would be healed. There seemed to be nothing for which to ask God. Surely there was no need of asking for His Presence; that Presence was all around me. So my prayer took the form of simply thanking Him for the miracle that His love could be such a personal love; for His tender care of Peter and Wee Peter and me.

At 8:15 the same morning, Peter stepped across the boundary that divides this life from the next. Then I knew that the experience of the night before had meant something far different. I had been granted it so that when the blow fell I might have the certainty that a loving Father had not deserted me.

Catherine Marshall

On a Sundial

With warning hand I mark Time's rapid flight
From Life's glad morning to its solemn night;
Yet, through the dear Lord's love, I also show
There's light above me by the shadow I throw.

John Greenleaf Whittier

GOLDEN NUGGETS

If the Father deigns to touch with Divine power the cold and pulseless heart of the buried acorn and to make it burst forth from its prison walls, will He leave neglected in the earth the soul of man made in the image of his Creator?

William Jennings Bryant

I shall grow old, but never lose life's zest,
Because the road's last turn will be the best.

Henry Van Dyke

In Old Age

Victor Hugo, author of Les Miserables and one of the great figures of literature, was born on February 26, 1802. He died in 1885 at the age of 83. He wrote of his aging:

"When I go down to the grave, I can say like many others, 'I have finished my day's work,' but I cannot say, 'I have finished my life.' My day's work will begin again the next morning; the tomb is not a blind alley, it is a thoroughfare. It closes on the twilight. It opens on the dawn."

The Golden City

(From Part I of The Pilgrim's Progress)

Now, when they were come up to the gate, there was written over it, in letters of gold,

"BLESSED ARE THEY THAT DO HIS COMMANDMENTS, THAT THEY MAY HAVE RIGHT TO THE TREE OF LIFE, AND MAY ENTER IN THROUGH THE GATES INTO THE CITY"

Now I saw in my dream, that these two men went in at the gate, and, lo! as they entered, they were transfigured; and they had raiment put on, that shone like gold. There were also that met them with harps and crowns, and gave them to them; the harps to praise withal, and the crowns in token of honour. Then I heard in my dream, that all the *bells* in the City rang again for joy, and that it was said unto them, ENTER YE INTO THE JOY OF OUR LORD. I also heard the men themselves, that they sang with a loud voice, saying,

"BLESSING, AND HONOUR, AND GLORY, AND POWER BE UNTO HIM THAT SITTETH UPON THE THRONE, AND UNTO THE LAMB, FOR EVER AND EVER."

Now, just as the gates were opened to let in the men, I looked in after them, and behold the City shone like the sun; the streets also were paved with gold; and in them walked many men with crowns on their heads, palms in their hands, and golden harps, to sing praises withal.

There were also of them that had wings, and they answered one another without intermission, saying, "Holy, holy, holy is he Lord." And after that they shut up the gates; which when I had seen, I wished myself among them.

Now, while I was gazing upon all these things, I turned my head to look back, and saw Ignorance come up the river-side: but he soon got over, and that without half the difficulty which the other two men met with. For it happened that there was then in that place one Vain-hope, a ferryman, that with his boat helped him over: so he, as the others I saw, did ascend the hill, to come up to the gate; only he came alone neither did any man meet him with the least encouragement. When he was come up to the gate, he looked up to the writing that was above, and then began to knock, supposing that entrance should have been quickly administered to him: but he was asked by the men that looked over the top of the gate, Whence come you? and what would you have? He answered, I have eat and drunk in the presence of the King, and he has taught in our streets. Then they asked him for his certificate, that they might go in and show it to the King: so he fumbled in his bosom for one, and found none. Then said they, Have you none? but the man answered never a word. So they told the King, but he would not come down to see him, but commanded the two shining ones, that conducted Christian and Hopeful to the City, to go out, and take Ignorance, and bind him hand and foot, and have him away. Then they took him up, and carried him through the air to the door that I saw in the side of the hill, and put him in there. Then I saw that there was a way to hell, even from the gates of heaven, as well as from the city of Destruction. So I awoke, and behold it was a dream.

John Bunyan

The Shadows Of The Evening Hours

The shadows of the evening hours
Fall from the darkening sky;
Upon the fragrance of the flowers
The dews of evening lie:
Before Thy throne, O Lord of heaven,
We kneel at close of day;
Look on Thy children from on high,
And hear us while we pray.

Slowly the rays of daylight fade:
So fade within our heart
The hopes in earthly love and joy,
That one by one depart.
Slowly the bright stars, one by one
Within the heavens shine:
Give us, O Lord, fresh hopes in heav'n,
And thrust in things divine.

Let peace, O Lord, Thy peace, O God,
Upon our souls descend;
From midnight fears and perils, Thou
Our trembling hearts defend.
Give us a respite from our toil,
Calm and subdue our woes;
Through the long day we labor, Lord,
O give us now repose.

Adelaide A. Procter

Afterglow

The day died in a flood of crimson flame
That bathed the hills in beauty richly rare.
All the world bowed down
And I, too, came to stand and wonder in worship there.

Then a small voice seemed to question me,
When death shall come and I must gladly go,
Will there be someone to love my memory?
Oh, Lord, shall I, too, leave an afterglow?

Author Unknown

Surely God would not have created such a being as man, with an ability to grasp the infinite, to exist only for a day! No, no, man was made for immortality.

Abraham Lincoln

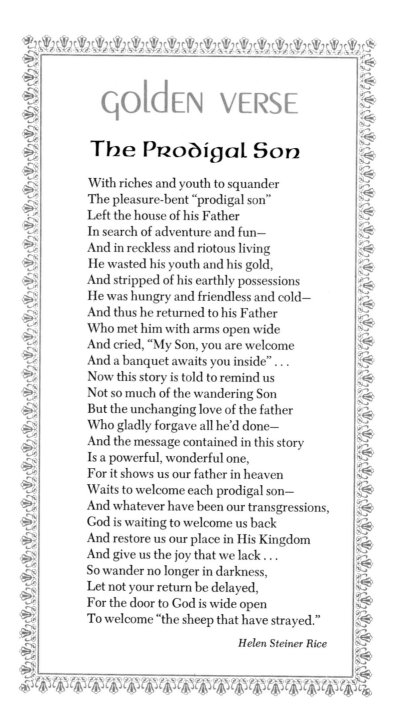

GOLDEN VERSE

The Prodigal Son

With riches and youth to squander
The pleasure-bent "prodigal son"
Left the house of his Father
In search of adventure and fun—
And in reckless and riotous living
He wasted his youth and his gold,
And stripped of his earthly possessions
He was hungry and friendless and cold—
And thus he returned to his Father
Who met him with arms open wide
And cried, "My Son, you are welcome
And a banquet awaits you inside" . . .
Now this story is told to remind us
Not so much of the wandering Son
But the unchanging love of the father
Who gladly forgave all he'd done—
And the message contained in this story
Is a powerful, wonderful one,
For it shows us our father in heaven
Waits to welcome each prodigal son—
And whatever have been our transgressions,
God is waiting to welcome us back
And restore us our place in His Kingdom
And give us the joy that we lack . . .
So wander no longer in darkness,
Let not your return be delayed,
For the door to God is wide open
To welcome "the sheep that have strayed."

Helen Steiner Rice

Let not your heart be troubled: ye believe in God, believe also in me. In my Father's house are many mansions: if it were not so, I would have told you. I go to prepare a place for you. And if I go and prepare a place for you, I will come again, and receive you unto myself; that where I am, there ye may be also. And whither I go ye know, and the way ye know. Thomas saith unto him, Lord, we know not whither thou goest; and how can we know the way? Jesus saith unto him, I am the way, the truth, and the life: no man cometh unto the Father, but by me. If ye had known me, ye should have known my Father also: and from henceforth ye know him, and have seen him. Philip saith unto him, Lord, shew us the Father, and it sufficeth us. Jesus saith unto him, Have I been so long time with you, and yet hast thou not known me, Philip? He that hath seen me hath seen the Father; and how sayest thou then, Shew us the Father? Believeth thou not that I am in the Father, and the Father in me? The words that I speak unto you I speak not of myself: but the Father that dwelleth in me, he doeth the works. Believe me that I am in the Father, and the Father in me: or else believe me for the very works' sake. Verily, verily, I say unto you, He that believeth on me, the works that I do shall he do also; and greater works than these shall he do: because I go unto my Father. And whatsoever ye shall ask in my name, that will I do, that the Father may be glorified in the Son. If ye shall ask anything in my name, I will do it. If ye love me, keep my commandments. And I will pray the Father, and He shall give you another Comforter, that he may abide with you for ever; Even the Spirit of truth whom the world cannot receive, because it seeth him not, neither knoweth him: but ye know him; for he dwelleth with you, and shall be in you. I will not leave you comfortless: I will come to you. Yet a little while, and the world seeth me no more; but ye see me: because I live, ye shall live also. At that day ye shall know that I am in my Father, and ye in me, and I in you. He that hath my commandments, and keepeth them, he it is that loveth me: and he that loveth me shall be loved of my Father, and I will love him, and I will manifest myself to him. Judas saith unto him, not Iscariot, Lord, how is it that thou wilt manifest thyself unto us, and not unto the world? Jesus answered and said unto him, If a man love me, he will keep my words: and my Father will love him, and we will come unto him, and make our abode with him. He that loveth me not keepeth not my sayings: and the word which ye hear is not mine, but the Father's which sent me. These things have I spoken unto you, being yet present with you. But the Comforter, which is the Holy Ghost, whom the Father will send in my name, he shall teach you all things, and bring all things to your remembrance, whatsoever I have said unto you. Peace I leave with you, my peace I give unto you: not as the world giveth, give I unto you. Let not your heart be troubled, neither let it be afraid.

John 14:1-27

God Knows

God knows our sorrows, griefs, and cares,
Each secret thought and fear.
God knows how hard the road can be
Throughout each passing year.

God knows that every sinful heart
Can still repentant be.
God knows that every weary soul
Is longing to be free.

And when our life on earth is o'er,
His mercy then He shares.
He bids us lay our burdens down
Because He knows—and cares.

M. M. Duncan

From Darkness To Light

Death is not death if it kills no part of us, save
    that which hindered us from perfect life.
Death is not death if it raises us in a moment
    from darkness into light, from weakness
    into strength, from sinfulness into holiness.
Death is not death if it brings us nearer to
    Christ, who is the fount of life.
Death is not death if it perfects our faith by
    sight and lets us behold Him in whom we
    have believed.
Death is not death if it gives us to those whom
    we have loved and lost, for whom we have
    lived, for whom we long to live again.
Death is not death if it rids us of doubt and
    fear, of chance and change, of space and
    time, and all which space and time bring
    forth and then destroy.
Death is not death, for Christ has conquered
    Death for Himself and for those who trust
    in Him.

Charles Kingsley

The Death Of Little Nell

She was dead. No sleep so beautiful and calm, so free from trace of pain, so fair to look upon. She seemed a creature fresh from the hand of God, and waiting for the breath of life; not one who had lived, and suffered death. Her couch was dressed with here and there some winter berries and green leaves, gathered in a spot she had been used to favor. "When I die, put near me something that has loved the light, and had the sky above it always." These were her words.

She was dead. Dear, gentle, patient, noble Nell was dead. Her little bird, a poor, slight thing the pressure of a finger would have crushed, was stirring nimbly in its cage, and the strong heart of its child-mistress was mute and motionless forever! Where were the traces of her early cares, her sufferings, and fatigues? All gone. Sorrow was dead, indeed, in her; but peace and perfect happiness were born, imaged in her tranquil beauty and profound repose.

And still her former self lay there, unaltered in this change. Yes! the old fireside had smiled upon that same sweet face; it had passed, like a dream, through haunts of misery and care; at the door of the poor schoolmaster on the summer evening, before the furnace fire upon the cold wet night, at the still bedside of the dying boy, there had been the same mild and lovely look. So shall we know the angels, in their majesty, after death.

The old man held one languid arm in his, and had the small hand tight folded to his breast for warmth. It was the hand she had stretched out to him with her last smile; the hand that had led him on through all their wanderings. Ever and anon he pressed it to his lips; then hugged it to his breast again, murmuring that it was warmer now, and as he said it, he looked in agony to those who stood around, as if imploring them to help her.

"It is not," said the schoolmaster, as he bent down to kiss her on the cheek, and gave his tears free vent, "It is not in *this* world that heaven's justice ends. Think what earth is, compared with the world to which her young spirit has winged its early flight, and say, if one deliberate wish, expressed in solemn tones above this bed, could call her back to life, which of us would utter it?"

She had been dead two days. They were all about her at the time, knowing that the end was drawing on. She died soon after day-break. They had read and talked to her in the earlier portion of the night; but, as the hours crept on, she sank to sleep. They could tell by what she faintly uttered in her dreams, that they were of her journeyings with the old man; they were of no painful scenes, but of the people who had helped them, and used them kindly; for she often said "God bless you!" with great fervor.

Waking, she had never wandered in her mind but once, and that was at beautiful music, which, she said, was in the air. God knows. It may have been. Opening her eyes, at last, from a very quiet sleep, she begged that they would kiss her once again. That done, she turned to the old man, with a lovely smile upon her face, such, they said, as they had never seen, and could never forget, and clung, with both her arms, about his neck. She had never murmured or complained; but, with a quiet mind, and manner quite unaltered, save that she every day became more earnest and more grateful to them, faded like the light upon the summer's evening.

Charles Dickens (From The Old Curiosity Shop)

(ACKNOWLEDGMENTS continued from page IV)

Robert Frost, "Stopping By Woods On A Snowy Evening," from THE POETRY OF ROBERT FROST edited by Edward Connery Lathem. Copyright © 1923, © 1969 by Holt, Rinehart and Winston, Inc. Copyright © 1951 by Robert Frost. Reprinted by permission of Holt, Rinehart and Winston, Inc.

Ethel Romig Fuller, "Today," from KITCHEN SONNETS. Reprinted by permission of Binfords and Mort, Publishers.

Billy Graham, "Easter," from PEACE WITH GOD. Copyright © 1953 by Billy Graham. Reprinted by permission of Doubleday and Co., Inc.

Eileen Gruder, an excerpt from TO LIVE IN LOVE. Copyright © 1967 by Zondervan Publishers. Reprinted with permission.

Edgar Guest, "Myself," "The Mother's Question," and "How Do You Tackle Your Work," from THE COLLECTED VERSE OF EDGAR GUEST. Copyright © 1934 by Reilly, Lee and Sons. Used with permission.

Alma Robison Higbee, "January Snow," from WHO TELLS THE CROCUSES IT'S SPRING. Reprinted by special permission of Farm Journal, Inc. Copyright © 1971, Countryside Press.

Donna Hosford, "Fenestralia," from GOD, I LIKE YOU by Sherwood Wirt and Charlene Anderson. Copyright © 1962, 68, 69, 70, by The Billy Graham Evangelistic Assn. Used with permission.

Will Houghton, an excerpt from LET'S GO BACK TO THE BIBLE, by Will Houghton. Reprinted by permission of Fleming H. Revell Company.

Albert P. Hout, "A Little Human Happiness," from THE LION, May 1971. As condensed in the October, 1971 READER'S DIGEST. Copyright © 1971 by Lions International and The Reader's Digest Assn., Inc. Used with permission.

James Weldon Johnson, "Lift Every Voice and Sing," from LIFT EVERY VOICE AND SING by James W. and Rosamund Johnson. Copyright © 1970 by Hawthorn Books, Inc. Reprinted by permission of Hawthorn Books, Inc., New York.

Muriel Schrader Mann, "When Comes The Time," from CHRISTIANITY TODAY. Reprinted by permission of CHRISTIANITY TODAY.

Catherine Marshall, "To Comfort All That Mourn," from TO LIVE AGAIN. Copyright © 1957 by Catherine Marshall. Reprinted by permission of McGraw-Hill Book Co.

Helen Lowrie Marshall, "Especially For You," "A Faith To Live By," "Candlelight and Starlight," "Always There," "A Lovely Day," "My Day," "An Ordinary Day," and "On A Lonely Hill," from HOLD TO YOUR DREAM. Copyright © 1965 by Helen Lowrie Marshall. Reprinted by permission of Doubleday and Company, Inc.

Peter Marshall, a prayer from THE PRAYERS OF PETER MARSHALL. Copyright © 1949, 50, 51, 54, by Catherine Marshall. Used with permission.

Roy O. McClain, "The Hidden Hand of God," from IF WITH ALL YOUR HEART. Reprinted by permission of Fleming H. Revell Co.

Paul McElroy, "Living by Grace." Reprinted by permission of Peter Pauper Press.

Jane Merchant, "To Know Him Who Is True," from THINK ABOUT THESE THINGS. Copyright © 1956 by Pierce and Wasabaugh (Abingdon Press); "My Thanks To Thee," from PETALS OF LIGHT. Copyright © 1961 by Abingdon Press; "One Day For Thanks," from WHO TELLS THE CROCUSES IT'S SPRING. Reprinted by special permission of Farm Journal, Inc Copyright © 1971, Countryside Press.

James J. Metcalfe, "Keep Praying," from POEM PORTRAITS FOR ALL OCCASIONS. Reprinted by permission of Doubleday and Kristina Metcalfe Lewis.

Minnie Hite Moody, "Questions For The First Day of School," from WHO TELLS THE CROCUSES IT'S SPRING. Reprinted by special permission of Farm Journal, Inc. Copyright © 1971, Countryside Press.

Grandma Moses, "The Good Old Days," from pages 139-140 of GRANDMA MOSES, MY LIFE'S HISTORY edited by Otto Kallir. Copyright © 1952 by Grandma Moses Properties, Inc. Used by permission of Harper and Row, Publishers.

Lois Kingsley Pelton, "Lonely Farm," from WHO TELLS THE CROCUSES IT'S SPRING. Reprinted by special permission of Farm Journal, Inc. Copyright © 1971, Countryside Press.

John W. Peterson, "Drink Deep, My Soul," from FAVORITE POEMS. Copyright © 1963 by Singspiration, Inc. All rights reserved. Used by permission.

Caryl Porter, "Wonder Lies In A Round Rainbow," from TOGETHER, May 1972. Copyright © 1972 by The Methodist Publishing House. Used by permission.

Eugenia Price, "Anna," from THE UNIQUE WORLD OF WOMEN. Copyright © 1969 by Zondervan Publishers.

"The Freedom Of Love," from MAKE LOVE YOUR AIM. Copyright © 1967 by Eugenia Price. Used with permission.

Dale Evans Rogers, "My Pilot," from NO TWO WAYS ABOUT IT. Reprinted by permission of Fleming H. Revell Company.

Archibald Rutledge, a selection from LIFE'S EXTRAS. Reprinted by permission of Fleming H. Revell Company.

Clyta Shaw, "Simile," from GOD, I LIKE YOU by Sherwood Wirt and Charlene Anderson. Copyright © 1962, 68, 69, 70, by The Billy Graham Evangelistic Assn. Used with permission.

E-Yeh-Shure, "Beauty," from I AM A PUEBLO INDIAN GIRL. Copyright © 1939 by William Morrow & Co.; renewed 1967, by Louise Abeita Chiwiwi. Used by permission.

Carol Spencer, "The Whole Bit," from GOD, I LIKE YOU by Sherwood Wirt and Charlene Anderson. Copyright © 1962, 68, 69, 70, by The Billy Graham Evangelistic Assn. Used with permission.

Nancy Spiegelberg, "Problem," from GOD, I LIKE YOU by Sherwood Wirt and Charlene Anderson. Copyright © 1962, 68, 69, 70, by The Billy Graham Evangelistic Assn. Used with permission.

Velma West Sykes, "Christmas Parable," from WHO TELLS THE CROCUSES IT'S SPRING. Reprinted by special permission of Farm Journal, Inc. Copyright © 1971, Countryside Press.

Perry Tanksley, "The Key To Friendship," from LOVE GIFT. Reprinted by permission of Fleming H. Revell Company.

Floyd W. Tompkins, a prayer from PRAYERS FOR THE QUIET HOUR. Reprinted by permission of The American Sunday School Union, Philadelphia, Pa.

John Townsend Trowbridge, "Midwinter," from POETICAL WORKS OF JOHN TOWNSEND TROWBRIDGE. Reprinted by permission of Houghton Mifflin Co.

Fritz Vincken, "Truce In The Forest," from THE READER'S DIGEST, January, 1973. Copyright © 1972 by The Reader's Digest Assn., Inc.

Myra Brooks Welch, "The Breath of God," from THE TOUCH OF THE MASTER'S HAND. Reprinted by permission of Brethren Press, Elgin, Ill.

W. Beran Wolfe, "The Happy Man," from HOW TO BE HAPPY THOUGH HUMAN. Used by permission of Holt, Rinehart and Winston Company, Inc.

WE ALSO WISH TO THANK

the following contributors and sources for their permission to reprint selections in this book:

Velta Myrle Allen, Viola J. Berg, Bruce Catton, CHRISTIANITY TODAY, E. Margaret Clarkson, Christine Grant Curless, DECISION, M. M. Duncan, Maude Durfee, Grace Easley, Elaine V. Emans, Alice Reynolds Flower, Lawerence R. Giles, Mrs. Arthur Guiterman, Harper and Row, for an excerpt from LOVE SONG, AUGUSTINE'S CONFESSIONS, by Sherwood Wirt, Pauline Havard, Victoria Saffelle Johnson, Hilda Mary Kerrigan, Dian Kilby, LADIES' HOME JOURNAL, THE LINK, Jerry Lipman, Harriet McLuckie, Corinna Marsh, PRESBYTERIAN LIFE, Provence-Jarrad Co., Helen Steiner Rice, Margaret Sangster, SUNSHINE Magazine, THESE TIMES, William Arthur Ward, WORLD VISION, Esther Baldwin York.

The following authors whose addresses we were unable to locate:

Catherine Berry, F. E. Elwell, Virginia Hibbard, Eleanor Hilleman, Howard Hopper, Franklin E. Jordan, Edgar Daniel Kramer, Clifton Rash, Gertrude Wiebe.

Diligent effort has been made to locate and secure permission for the inclusion of all copyrighted material in this book. If any such acknowledgments have been inadvertently omitted, the compilers and publishers would appreciate receiving full information so that proper credit may be given in future editions.